ADVANCED ENGLISH

Course Book

Level 8

SCHOLASTIC
New York Toronto London Auckland
Sydney New Delhi Hong Kong

Published by Scholastic India Pvt. Ltd.
A subsidiary of Scholastic Inc., New York, 10012 (USA)
Publishers since 1920, with international operations in Canada, Australia, New Zealand, the United Kingdom, India, and Hong Kong.

For information regarding permission, write to:
Scholastic India Pvt. Ltd.
Golf View Corporate Tower-A, 3rd Floor,
DLF Phase V, Gurgaon 122002 (India)

Series editor: Aishwarya Subramanian
Layout, design and typesetting by Ram Das Lal

First edition: October 2010
Reprint: January 2011, September 2011,March 2012

ISBN-13: 978-81-8477-499-3

Printed at: Shivam Offset Press, Noida

The Lexile measure represents the complexity of the text. This Lexile measure—along with other characteristics of the text, such as developmental level and subject matter—helps in selecting books that best match a reader's level and goals. For more information on using Lexile measures to connect readers with text, visit www.Lexile.com.

Contents

A Child's Right to Read	5
Detailed Table of Contents	6
Introduction	8
Friendship	
Friendship Sonnet	13
The Happy Prince	17
Communication	
Under a Telephone Pole	29
Talking to Jason	32
The Power of Hearing	40
The World	
Two Myths about Fire	51
Yogurt and Cinnamon Dessert with Rose Geraniums and Peach	57
27 Nisbat Road	61
Art and Culture	
Music	73
My Last Duchess	76
What is My Single Life Worth?	81

War and Peace

The Tenth Day 89

The Battle of Blenheim 100

Mysteries

The Purloined Letter 109

The Secret 119

The Future

The World in Your Room 127

There Will Come Soft Rains 136

The Story Collector 139

Acknowledgements 153

Evaluation Table 156

believe that LITERACY – the ability to READ, WRITE and UNDERSTAND – is the BIRTHRIGHT of every child in the ld as well as the pathway to SUCCEED in school and to realize a complete life. Young people need to read NONFICTION for ORMATION to understand their world, and LITERATURE for IMAGINATION to understand themselves. • We believe that the sive amounts of DIGITAL information and IMAGES now transmitted daily make it even more important for a young person to w how to ANALYZE, INTERPRET and understand information, to separate FACT from OPINION, and to have deep RESPECT LOGICAL THINKING. • We believe that literature and DRAMA, whether on printed pages, screens, on stage or film, help ng people EXPERIENCE the GREAT STORIES of EMOTION and ACTION, leading to a deeper UNDERSTANDING of what it ans to be TRULY HUMAN. Without this literacy heritage, life lacks MEANING, COHERENCE and SOUL. • We believe every d has a right to a "textual lineage" – a reading and writing autobiography which shows that WHO YOU ARE is in part developed ugh the STORIES and INFORMATION you've experienced. This textual lineage will enable all young people to have a READING D WRITING IDENTITY which helps them understand who they are and how they can MAKE THEIR LIVES BETTER. In short, U ARE WHAT YOU READ." • We believe every child should have ACCESS to books, magazines, newspapers, computers,

A Child's Right to Read

aders, and text on phones. Whatever way you read, you will need to figure out what the FACTS are or what the STORY tells No matter how and where you get access to IDEAS, you will need the SKILLS of READING to UNDERSTAND yourself YOUR WORLD. • We believe that reading WIDELY and reading FLUENTLY will give children the reading STAMINA to with more CHALLENGING texts they will meet in college, at work and in everyday LIFE. And every child should be able HOOSE and own the books they want to read, for that choice builds LITERACY CONFIDENCE – the ability to read, ITE and SPEAK about what they know, what they feel, and who they are. • We believe that every child has the right to a great her who will help them LEARN to read and LOVE TO READ. Children need teachers who provide INTENTIONAL, focused RUCTION to give young people the skills to read and INTERPRET INFORMATION or UNDERSTAND GREAT STORIES they encounter throughout life. • We believe that in the 21st century, the ability to read is NECESSARY not only to SUCCEED but URVIVE—for the ability to UNDERSTAND information and the POWER of stories is the key to a life of PURPOSE and MEANING.

Friendship	Lesson	Reading Comprehension	Vocabulary
	Friendship sonnet	Questions and answers	Sonnets
	The Happy Prince (840L)	Questions and answers	Odd word out
Communication	**Lesson**	**Reading Comprehension**	**Vocabulary**
	Under a Telephone Pole	Questions and answers	Homonyms
	Talking to Jason (730L)	Questions and answers	Completing a Crossw
	The Power of Hearing (1120L)	Questions and answers	Acronyms
The World	**Lesson**	**Reading Comprehension**	**Vocabulary**
	Two Myths About Fire (910L)	Questions and answers	Gods from different r
	Yogurt and Cinnamon Dessert with Rose Geraniums and Peach	Questions and answers	Collocations
	27 Nisbat Road (1180L)	Questions and answers	Words about cities
Art and Culture	**Lesson**	**Reading Comprehension**	**Vocabulary**
	Music	Questions and answers	Musical instrument
	My Last Duchess	Questions and answers	Archaic English
	What is My Single Life Worth? (1000L)	Questions and answers	Synonyms
War and Peace	**Lesson**	**Reading Comprehension**	**Vocabulary**
	The Tenth Day	Questions and answers	War idioms
	The Battle of Blenheim	Questions and answers	Forming new words longer word
Mysteries	**Lesson**	**Reading Comprehension**	**Vocabulary**
	The Purloined Letter	Questions and answers	Famous fictional de
	The Secret	Questions and answers	Alliteration and Re in poetry
The Future	**Lesson**	**Reading Comprehension**	**Vocabulary**
	The World in Your Room (1280L)	Questions and answers	Unscrambling wor
	There Will Come Soft Rains	Questions and answers	Pathetic fallacy
	The Story Collector (900L)	Questions and answers	Neologism

Grammar	**Writing**	Making connections between lessons Describing things Independent research
Conjunctions	Writing from a particular perspective	
Grammar	**Writing**	Making connections between lessons Class debate on modern communications technology Independent research
Clauses	Writing a character sketch	
Colons	Describing sounds	
Grammar	**Writing**	Making connections between lessons Listening to a story and answering questions Independent research
Modal verbs	Retelling myths and legends	
	Descriptive paragraph writing	
Gerunds	Writing a movie review	
Grammar	**Writing**	Analysis of chapters in relation to the broader theme Reading out loud Independent research
Infinitives	Expressing an opinion	
Grammar	**Writing**	Making connections between lessons Reading a poem in an expressive manner Independent research
Gerunds and infinitives	Writing a book review	
	Describing someone	
	Writing	Making connections between lessons Analysis of a genre Playing "Twenty Questions" Independent research
	Writing an informal letter	
Grammar	**Writing**	Making connections between chapters Research and presentation on an issue Independent research
Split infinitives	Describing an invention	
	Arguing a particular position	

Introduction

Advanced English is a series of coursebooks, workbooks and literature readers for students of classes 6, 7 and 8. The books are based on the current NCERT curriculum. The series uses a communicative approach to help students improve their written and verbal skills, and to foster a deeper appreciation of the English language.

In addition, the books aim to foster a love of literature and reading in children.

Advanced English has been designed to cover the essential skills of the language:

Language development	Communication skills	Social and other skills
• Reading comprehension	• Writing	• Debate
• Vocabulary	• Listening	• Activities
• Grammar	• Speaking	• Independent research

Some of the unique features of the series are:

Lexile measures

The Lexile framework for reading was created by Metametrics, the educational research organisation. Lexile measures assess the difficulty level of a piece of writing. Scholastic's coursebooks and supplementary readers have been lexiled by Metametrics. All the texts in these books are within or slightly above the recommended range of lexile scores for that age group. This means that the texts are of a level accessible to the students, yet still challenging.

Continuous and Comprehensive Evaluation

The CBSE describes CCE as a "system of school-based assessment that covers all aspects of student's development. It emphasizes two-fold objectives: continuity in evaluation and assessment of broad-based learning." The CBSE recommends the implementation of CCE after class 9, but the principle of broad-based learning is one that we believe should be implemented throughout the school career. To that end we have included a table at the back of the book which will allow teachers to evaluate the student's progress on a number of parameters at regular intervals throughout the year.

Selection of texts

The coursebook features a diverse selection of works by major Indian and international authors. There are stories, poems, plays, speeches and articles that are diverse in both genre and style.

Themed sections

The lessons are divided by theme, based on NCERT recommendations. Each theme features a relevant quote and a page for further exploring the links between the lessons and the theme. The book aims to encourage the students to make connections across chapters, and to identify and discuss broader issues. To this end, the theme pages also include further discussion, listening and speaking exercises in which the students are given debate topics and ideas to discuss.

Encouragement of independent thought and expression

Advanced English encourages students to form and defend opinions. The reading comprehension and further discussion sections contain a number of open-ended questions to which there is no definitive right or wrong answer. The listening and speaking exercises also provide the students encourage debate and active participation in the classroom. A variety of creative writing exercises give the students further practice in expressing their thoughts with originality and clarity.

Acquiring tools for independent learning

Through the learn more and activities sections, the students are encouraged to research specific subjects by themselves. The theme-based approach further enhances critical thinking skills, while a number of vocabulary exercises call for the use of the dictionary or thesaurus.

Attractive, "grown-up" format

The unusual size and layout of the book signify the students' transition from primary to middle school. The inclusion of high-quality black-and-white artwork further enhances the appeal of the book, making the reading experience more enjoyable.

Rigorous and challenging exercises

The vocabulary and grammar sections are accompanied by practice exercises. Further practice exercises can be found in the workbook.

Art and literature have always shared a symbiotic relationship. Such a cross-pollination of genres not only enriches the former, but informs the latter. Many visual learners will find that these connections allow for better retention of the material and enable an engagement that is above mere rote-learning. It is for this reason that we chose to use cover images based on the work of some of the world's great artists. The cover for this book is based on Claude Monet's "Woman with a Parasol – Madame Monet and Her Son". Monet lived from 1840-1926 and was one of the founders of French Impressionist painting. Some of his most famous works are "Impression, Sunrise", "Poppies Blooming" and "Bridge Over a Pond of Water Lilies".

FRIENDSHIP

"Friendship is born at that moment when one person says to another, 'What! You too? I thought I was the only one'."

—C.S. Lewis

1 Friendship Sonnet

William Shakespeare *(1564–1616) was an English poet and playwright. He is the most famous and possibly the greatest writer in English.*

When to the sessions of sweet silent thought
I **summon** up remembrance of things past,
I sigh the lack of many a thing I sought,
And with old **woes** new **wail** my dear time's waste:
Then can I drown an eye, unused to flow,
For precious friends hid in death's dateless night,
And weep afresh love's long since cancell'd woe,
And moan the expense of many a vanish'd sight:
Then can I grieve at **grievances foregone**,
And heavily from woe to woe tell o'er
The sad account of fore-bemoaned moan,
Which I new pay as if not paid before.
But if the while I think on thee, dear friend,
All losses are restored and sorrows end.

Reading Comprehension

1 Answer the following questions.

i What causes the poet to think about the past?

ii "Then can I drown an eye, unused to flow." What does this line mean?

iii What has happened to the "precious friends"?

iv Has the poet mourned over these grievances before? What makes you think so?

v "Which I new pay as if not paid before." In what way has the poet paid?

vi What causes the poet to feel happy once more?

summon: make an effort to produce (a particular quality or reaction) from within oneself
woes: great sorrow or distress
wail: feel deep sorrow for
grievances: real or imagined cause for complaint
foregone: past

Vocabulary

Sonnet

> A **sonnet** is a form of poem which is fourteen lines long. There are various types of sonnets. In a Shakespearian sonnet, the rhyme scheme is as follows:
> a-b-a-b, c-d-c-d, e-f-e-f, g-g; the last two lines rhyme with each other.

1 Read the examples of sonnets given here and work out their rhyme schemes.

i Death, be not proud, though some have callèd thee
Mighty and dreadful, for thou art not so;
For those whom thou think'st thou dost overthrow
Die not, poor death, nor yet canst thou kill me.
From rest and sleep, which yet thy pictures be,
Much pleasure, then from thee much more, must low
And soonest our best men with thee do go,
Rest of their bones and soul's delivery.
Thou art slave to fate, chance, kings and desperate men
And dost with poison, war and sickness dwell,
And poppy or charms can make us sleep as well
And better than thy stroke; why swell'st thou then ?
One short sleep past, we wake eternally,
And death shall be no more; death, thou shalt die.

—John Donne ("Death Be Not Proud")

ii Scorn not the Sonnet; Critic, you have frowned,
Mindless of its just honours; with this key

Shakespeare unlocked his heart; the melody
Of this small lute gave ease to Petrarch's wound;
A thousand times this pipe did Tasso sound;
With it Camoens soothed an exile's grief;
The Sonnet glittered a gay myrtle leaf
Amid the cypress with which Dante crowned
His visionary brow: a glow-worm lamp,
It cheered mild Spenser, called from Faery-land
To struggle through dark ways; and when a damp
Fell round the path of Milton, in his hand
The Thing became a trumpet; whence he blew
Soul-animating strains—alas, too few!

—William Wordsworth ("Scorn Not the Sonnet")

iii A hint of rain—a touch of lazy doubt—
Sent me to bedward on that prime of nights,
When the air met and burst the aerolites,
Making the men stare and the children shout:
Why did no beam from all that rout and rush
Of darting meteors, pierce my drowsed head?
Strike on the portals of my sleep? and flush
My spirit through mine eyelids, in the stead
Of that poor vapid dream? My soul was pained,
My very soul, to have slept while others woke,
While little children their delight outspoke,
And in their eyes' small chambers entertained
Far notions of the Kosmos! I mistook
The purpose of that night—it had not rained.

—Charles Tennyson Turner ("Missing the Meteors")

2 The Happy Prince

***Oscar Wilde** (1854–1900) was an Irish writer and poet. He is best known for his novel* The Picture of Dorian Gray *and his plays* The Importance of Being Earnest *and* An Ideal Husband.

High above the city, on a tall column, stood the statue of the Happy Prince. He was **gilded** all over with thin leaves of fine gold, for eyes he had two bright sapphires, and a large red ruby glowed on his sword-hilt. He was very much admired indeed.

One night there flew over the city a little Swallow. His friends had gone away to Egypt six weeks before, but he had stayed behind. All day long he flew, and at nighttime he arrived at the city. Then he saw the statue on the tall column.

"I will put up there," he cried, "'it is a fine position, with plenty of fresh air." So he alighted just between the feet of the Happy Prince.

"I have a golden bedroom," he said softly to himself as he looked round, and he prepared to go to sleep; but just as he was putting his head under his wing a large drop of water fell on him. "What a curious thing!" he cried, "there is not a single cloud in the sky, the stars are quite clear and bright, and yet it is raining."

He looked up, and saw—Ah! What did he see?

The eyes of the Happy Prince were filled with tears, and tears were running down his golden cheeks. His face was so beautiful in the moonlight that the little Swallow was filled with pity.

"Who are you?" he said.

"I am the Happy Prince."

"Why are you weeping then?" asked the Swallow; "you have quite drenched me."

"When I was alive and had a human heart," answered the statue, "I did not know what tears were. And now that I am dead they have set

---

gilded: covered with thin leaves of gold

me up here so high that I can see all the ugliness and all the misery of my city, and I cannot choose but weep."

"Far away," continued the statue in a low musical voice, "far away in a little street there is a poor house. One of the windows is open, and through it I can see a woman seated at a table. Her face is thin and worn, and she has **coarse**, red hands, all pricked by the needle, for she is a **seamstress**. In a bed in the corner of the room, her little boy is lying ill. He has a fever, and is asking for oranges. His mother has nothing to give him but river water. Swallow, will you not bring her the ruby out of my sword-hilt? My feet are **fastened** to this pedestal and I cannot move."

"I am waited for in Egypt," said the Swallow. "My friends are flying up and down the Nile, and talking to the large lotus-flowers. Soon they will go to sleep in the tomb of the great King. The King is there himself in his painted coffin. He is wrapped in yellow linen, and embalmed with spices. Round his neck is a chain of pale green jade, and his hands are like withered leaves."

"Swallow, little Swallow," said the Prince, "will you not stay with me for one night, and be my messenger? The boy is so thirsty, and the mother so sad."

The Happy Prince looked so sad that the little Swallow was sorry. "It is very cold here," he said, "but I will stay with you for one night, and be your messenger."

"Thank you, little Swallow," said the Prince.

So the Swallow picked out the great ruby from the Prince's sword, and flew away with it in his beak over the roofs of the town.

He passed by the cathedral tower, where the white marble angels were sculptured. He passed over the river, and saw the lanterns hanging to the masts of the ships. At last he came to the poor house and looked in. The boy was tossing feverishly on his bed, and the mother had fallen asleep, she was so tired. In he hopped, and laid the great ruby on the table beside the woman's **thimble**. Then he flew gently round the bed, fanning the boy's forehead with his wings. "How

---

coarse: rough or harsh in texture
seamstress: a woman who sews, especially one who earns her living by sewing

fastened: fixed or held in a place
thimble: a small metal or plastic cap with a closed end, worn to protect the finger and push the needle in sewing

cool I feel," said the boy, "I must be getting better," and he sank into a delicious **slumber**.

Then the Swallow flew back to the Happy Prince, and told him what he had done. "It is curious," he remarked, "but I feel quite warm now, although it is so cold."

"That is because you have done a good action," said the Prince. And the little Swallow began to think, and then he fell asleep. Thinking always made him sleepy.

When day broke he flew down to the river and had a bath. "Tonight I go to Egypt," said the Swallow, and he was in high spirits at the prospect.

"Swallow, Swallow," said the Prince, "will you not stay with me one night longer?"

"I am waited for in Egypt," answered the Swallow. "Tomorrow my friends will fly up to the Second Cataract. The river-horse **couches** there among the **bulrushes**, and on a great granite throne sits the God Memnon. All night long he watches the stars, and when the morning star shines, he utters one cry of joy, and then he is silent. At noon the yellow lions come down to the water's edge to drink. They have eyes like green **beryls**, and their roar is louder than the roar of the cataract."

"Swallow, Swallow, little Swallow," said the Prince, "far away across the city I see a young man. He is leaning over a desk covered with papers. He has large and dreamy eyes. He is trying to finish a play for the Director of the Theatre, but he is too cold to write any more. There is no fire in the **grate**, and hunger has made him faint."

"I will wait with you one night longer," said the Swallow, who really had a good heart. "Shall I take him another ruby?"

"Alas! I have no ruby now," said the Prince; "my eyes are all that I have left. They are made of rare sapphires, which were brought out of India a thousand years ago. Pluck out one of them and take it to him."

"Dear Prince," said the Swallow, "I cannot do that"; and he began to weep.

---

slumber: sleep
couches: lay down
bulrushes: tall reed-like water plants with strap-like leaves and a dark brown velvety cylindrical head of numerous tiny flowers
beryls: transparent pale green, blue or yellow mineral consisting of a silicate of beryllium and aluminium, sometimes used as a gemstone
grate: the recess of a fireplace or furnace

"Swallow," said the Prince, "do as I command you."

So the Swallow plucked out the Prince's eye, and flew away to the student's **garret**.

The next day the Swallow flew down to the harbour. "I am going to Egypt!" cried the Swallow, but nobody minded, and when the moon rose he flew back to the Happy Prince.

"I am come to bid you goodbye," he cried.

"Swallow, little Swallow," said the Prince, "will you not stay with me one night longer?"

"It is winter," answered the Swallow, "and the chill snow will soon be here. Dear Prince, I must leave you, but I will never forget you."

"In the square below," said the Happy Prince, "there stands a little match-girl. She has let her matches fall in the gutter, and they are all spoiled. Her father will beat her if she does not bring home some money, and she is crying. Pluck out my other eye, and give it to her."

"I will stay with you one night longer," said the Swallow, "but I cannot pluck out your eye. You would be quite blind then."

"Swallow, said the Prince," "do as I command you."

So he plucked out the Prince's other eye, and darted down with it. He swooped past the match-girl, and slipped the jewel into the palm of her hand. "What a lovely bit of glass," cried the little girl and she ran home, laughing.

Then the Swallow came back to the Prince. "You are blind now," he said, "so I will stay with you always."

"No, little Swallow," said the poor Prince, "you must go away to Egypt."

"I will stay with you always," said the Swallow, and he slept at the Prince's feet.

"Dear little Swallow," said the Prince, "more marvellous than anything is the suffering of men and of women. There is no Mystery so great as Misery. Fly over my city, little Swallow, and tell me what you see there."

---

garret: a top -floor or attic room, especially a small dismal one

So the Swallow flew over the great city, and saw the rich making merry in their beautiful houses, while the beggars were sitting at the gates. He flew into dark lanes, and saw the white faces of starving children looking out **listlessly** at the black streets.

Then he flew back and told the Prince what he had seen.

"I am covered with fine gold," said the Prince, "you must take it off, leaf by leaf, and give it to my poor."

Leaf after leaf of the fine gold the Swallow picked off, till the Happy Prince looked quite dull and grey. Leaf after leaf of the fine gold he brought to the poor, and the children's faces grew rosier, and they laughed and played games in the street. "We have bread now!" they cried.

Then the snow came, and after the snow came the frost. The streets looked as if they were made of silver, they were so bright and glistening; long **icicles** like crystal daggers hung down from the eaves of the houses, everybody went about in furs, and the little boys wore scarlet caps and skated on the ice.

The poor little Swallow grew colder and colder, but he would not leave the Prince, he loved him too well. He picked up crumbs outside the baker's door when the baker was not looking and tried to keep himself warm by flapping his wings.

But at last he knew that he was going to die. "Goodbye, dear Prince!" he murmured, "Will you let me kiss your hand?"

"I am glad that you are going to Egypt at last, little Swallow," said the Prince, "you have stayed too long here; but you must kiss me, for I love you."

"It is not to Egypt that I am going," said the Swallow. And he kissed the Happy Prince on the lips, and fell down dead at his feet.

At that moment a curious crack sounded inside the statue, as if something had broken. The fact is that the leaden heart had snapped right in two. It certainly was a dreadfully hard frost.

Early the next morning the Mayor was walking in the square below in company with the Town Councillors. As they passed the column

---

listlessly: lacking in energy or enthusiasm

icicles: a hanging, tapering piece of ice formed by the freezing of dripping water he looked up at the statue: "Dear me! How shabby the Happy Prince looks!" he said.

"How shabby indeed!" cried the Town Councillors, who always agreed with the Mayor, and they went up to look at it.

"The ruby has fallen out of his sword, his eyes are gone, and he is golden no longer," said the Mayor, "In fact he is little better than a beggar!"

"Little better than a beggar," said the Town Councillors.

"And here is actually a dead bird at his feet!" continued the Mayor. "We must really issue a proclamation that birds are not to be allowed to die here." And the Town Clerk made a note of the suggestion.

So they pulled down the statue of the Happy Prince. Then they melted the statue in a **furnace**, and the Mayor held a meeting of the Corporation to decide what was to be done with the metal. "We must have another statue, of course," he said, "and it shall be a statue of myself."

"Of myself," said each of the Town Councillors, and they quarrelled. When I last heard of them they were quarrelling still.

"What a strange thing!" said the overseer of the workmen at the **foundry**. "This broken lead heart will not melt in the furnace. We must throw it away." So they threw it on a dust heap where the dead Swallow was also lying.

"Bring me the two most precious things in the city," said God to one of His Angels; and the Angel brought Him the leaden heart and the dead bird.

"You have rightly chosen," said God, "for in my garden of Paradise this little bird shall sing for evermore, and in my city of gold the Happy Prince shall praise me."

---

furnace: an enclosed structure in which material can be heated to very high temperatures

foundry: a workshop or factory where metal is cast

Reading Comprehension

1 Answer the following questions.

i Where had the Swallow's friends gone?

ii To whom was the ruby given?

iii What was the match-girl's reaction to the sapphire?

iv Why did the Swallow decide to stay with the Prince always?

v What strange thing did the overseer at the foundry discover?

vi Why did the Town Councillors quarrel?

vii What were the two most precious things in the city?

viii Why do you think the Prince "did not know what tears were" when he was alive?

ix What, according to the Prince, is the greatest mystery?

Vocabulary

1 Circle the odd word in the following sets of words.

i ruby sapphire emerald gold diamond amethyst topaz garnet

ii needle thimble pincushion thread stitch orange embroidery

iii Sudan Egypt France Algeria Ethiopia Nigeria Kenya

iii cathedral palace church temple mosque abbey synagogue

Grammar

Conjunctions

1 Join the following sentences using the conjunctions given in brackets.

i Samit got his salary. He bought his parents a new television. (after) After sent got his salary he...

ii They kept buying expensive things. They had no money. (even though)

iii Bhoomika shelled the peas. She was listening to music. (while)

iv You turn left at the end of the road. You will come to the park. (if)

v You cannot have any dessert. You have not finished your meal. (as)

vi You cannot have any dessert. You have finished your meal. (until)

vii You are going to the market. Please pick up Rohini's medicine from the chemist. (if)

viii It was hot. The ice cream melted before we could eat it! (so ... that)

Writing

The Swallow and the Happy Prince both watched the city from above. Imagine you were a bird flying above your school. Write a description of how the school would look to you.

Further Discussion

1 Do you think that either the poem or the story in this section are happy? How does the friendship of the characters help them?

2 Read the story "The Nightingale and the Rose" by Oscar Wilde in the Literature Reader. Like "The Happy Prince", this story is about a young man and a bird. In what ways are the two stories similar or different? Pay particular attention to their endings.

3 Discuss the portrayal of the town councillors in "The Happy Prince".

Listening and Speaking

The Happy Prince and the Swallow both describe what they see to each other. Describe something that you can see around you and ask your classmates to guess what it is.

Learn More

1. A number of scholars believe that the author and playwright Shakespeare never really existed. They feel that someone from his background would not have had the education or knowledge of history necessary to write such plays, so "William Shakespeare" must have been the pen-name of another writer. Below are some of the historical figures who people think might have been Shakespeare. What can you find out about them?

Christopher Marlowe	Sir Francis Bacon
Queen Elizabeth I	Edward de Vere, Earl of Oxford
William Stanley, Earl of Derby	Emilia Lanier

COMMUNICATION

"No pleasure has any savor for me without communication."
—Michel de Montaigne

3 Under a Telephone Pole

Carl Sandburg *(1878–1967) was an American writer and poet.*

I am a copper wire **slung** in the air,
Slim against the sun I make not even a clear line of shadow.
Night and day I keep singing—humming and **thrumming**:
It is love and war and money; it is the fighting and the tears, the work and want,
Death and laughter of men and women passing through me, carrier of your speech,
In the rain and the wet dripping, in the dawn and the shine drying,
A copper wire.

Reading Comprehension

1 Answer the following questions.
   i Who or what is the speaker?
   ii Why doesn't the wire make a clear line of shadow?
   iii What sort of news is transmitted over the wire?
   iv What do you notice about the structure of this poem? Do you think it should be called a poem?

Vocabulary

Homonyms

Homonyms are words which sound the same but have different meanings.

1 Fill in the blanks using the correct homonyms from the brackets.

   i The ball made a wide ____________ (ark/arc) through the air before landing in the palm of the fielder.

slung: loosely suspensed

thrumming: low, vibrating, humming noise

ii The terrified puppy ____________ (cowered/coward) in the corner as the young woman shouted.

iii Namrata was well trained in the ____________ (marshall/martial) arts, having a black belt to her credit.

iv Every politician has to ____________ (canvas/canvass) for votes.

v Charles has a herb garden where he grows sage, basil, mint and ____________ (thyme/time).

vi The children ____________ (pier/peer) over the wall at their new neighbour.

vii When the rope ____________ (phrase/frays) and breaks the bucket will tilt, spilling the sand.

viii A major flaw of our education system is the emphasis on ____________ (wrote/rote) learning.

4 Talking to Jason

Cynthia Lord *is a children's author. This chapter is an extract from her first novel* Rules.

The bell above the clinic door **jangles** and Mom looks up from the pages. "Hello, Elizabeth," she says to Jason's mother. "Hi, Jason."

Jason doesn't move his head, but his eyes turn to me. "Ahhh!"

I **flinch**. I know Jason can't help it, but sometimes the sounds he makes are loud and creepy.

Jason raps his communication book.

"My son wants to thank you for the picture you gave him," Mrs Morehouse says to me. "In fact, he asked me to hang it on his wall."

Jason's mouth drops open.

I give Jason my I-hate-it-when-my-mom-does-that-too eye roll.

He smiles and taps his book.

"Jason is wondering if he could have your name in his book?" Mrs Morehouse watches his hand move card to card. "So he can talk to you. Would you mind, Catherine?"

It seems weird to think of my name in some boy's communication book, but I don't know how I could say no, so I say, "Okay."

She takes a little card and a pen from her purse. Watching her, I wonder how that'd feel, to have to wait for someone to make a word before I could use it. And to have all my words lying out in the open, complete strangers able to walk by and see everything that mattered to me, without even knowing my name.

Jason **grimaces** at the card.

"Well, you know I can't draw," Mrs Morehouse says. "Do you want me to put her name without a picture?"

"I could draw it." Jeez! Where'd that come from? Just popped out of my mouth without checking with my brain first.

---

jangles: make or cause to make a ringing metallic sound, typically a discordant one
flinch: make a quick, nervous movement of the face or body as an instinctive reaction to fear or pain
grimaces: to have an ugly, twisted expression on one's face, typically expressing disgust, pain or wry amusement

"That'd be great." Mrs Morehouse pulls another blank card from her purse. "If you draw on this, it'll fit in his book."

On my way past Jason's wheelchair, I study a page of his communication book so my card'll match the others. About two inches square, each card has a simple black-and-white line drawing and the word or phrase printed along the top. His book has clear vinyl pages, like an album for trading cards, only with smaller pockets to fit the word cards.

Back at my spot on the couch, I ask Mom if I can borrow the little makeup mirror from her purse. I lay the mirror and the card on my sketchbook to give me something firm underneath while I draw.

Two inches wide, two inches high: a white block waiting for me to appear inside. But how should I look? Like my school picture, with

just-combed hair and my say-cheese smile? Or like I do at home, with ponytail hair and wearing my favourite purple T-shirt? I can't decide, so I do the easy part first and write "Catherine" at the top in tiny, neat letters.

I might not be the world's best artist, but I can draw better than the stick figures and line drawings on Jason's other cards, all perfect circles and ruler-straight lines. I choose a peach-coloured pencil and study my face in the mirror. I draw the slow curve of my right cheek, sweeping down to my too-pointy chin, up my other cheek, over the top of my head, and back to where my line began.

I draw how I usually look: brown ponytail, blue-grey eyes, wearing my purple T-shirt. Not a perfect circle or ruler-straight line anywhere.

Besides, Jason probably wouldn't recognise the school-picture me anyway.

But when Mrs Morehouse tries to slide my card into one of the little clear pockets in Jason's book, it's the tiniest bit too big. "I'll take a sliver off the side," she says, heading for the receptionist's desk. "Let me get some scissors."

Beside me, Jason taps.

"Excuse me!" I call to Mrs Morehouse's back. "He wants something!"

She doesn't even turn around. "Would you see what it is?"

I'm scared I won't understand Jason, but she's already chatting with the receptionist. Holding my breath, I peer down at his finger pointing to —

Thank you.

"Oh." I let go my breath. "You're welcome."

Mrs Morehouse trims my word to fit his book, and Jason lets out a loud "Ahhh!"

He says it so loud, Mrs Frost turns down her hearing aid.

Jason slaps, Good job.

My name stands out, colourful and detailed among the black-and-white plainness of his other cards. Sandwich. Pizza. Soda. Drink.

---

sliver: a small, thin, narrow piece of something cut or split off a larger piece

Eat. More. Good. Nice. Bad. Sad. Happy. Mad. Van. Want. Go. I'm sorry. No. Yes. Maybe. I don't know. Make. Tell. Help. Wait. Baseball. Music. Guitar. Piano. Like. Please. Thank you. Me too. Okay. Hi. Goodbye. Boy. Girl. Man. Woman. Picture. Word. Good job. What? Who? Why? And many more, all the way to Catherine.

I long to pull his cards out and add red to the van, yellow to the happy face, and thick purple jelly between the slices of bread in the sandwich. I want to show Jason I'm sorry for not-looking at him the same embarrassed way I hate people not-looking at David. But how? "If you ever want me to make you more words," I say, "just ask.".

"Thank you," Mrs Morehouse says, adjusting her earring. "But there's no need. These cards are part of a speech programme we use, and it comes with a whole book of words. I can copy whatever he needs from there."

Jason shorts his mother a what? look. Yes. More. Picture.

Mrs Morehouse sighs. "Are you sure you don't mind, Catherine?"

"I'm sure." I turn the pages of Jason's communication book, reading through his cards so I don't repeat the words or phrases he already has. Which shouldn't be hard, since all his words are boring. But to be polite, I ask his mother what words she suggests I make.

"Something you like would be nice. Then he could talk to you about it." She pulls a stack of blank cards from her purse. "Would seven be too many?"

"Seven's fine." Taking the cards, I'm not sure what to do. Go back to the couch? Stay here? Jason turns a page in his communication book and my insides twist. "Well." I glance at my watch. "Sorry, I — "

"HI JASON!" His speech **therapist** smiles, striding into the waiting room. "Am I interrupting something?"

I open my mouth to say no, but she's already looking past me. "How's his day been going?"

Jason taps, Good.

"He's been a bit **cranky**," Mrs Morehouse says. "I think he stayed up too late last night watching the **Red Sox**. It went to extra innings."

---

therapist: a person skilled in a particular kind of therapy
cranky: bad-tempered; irritable

Red Sox: an American baseball team

"Oh? ARE YOU" (points to Jason) "CRANKY?" (gesture plus crabby face).

Jason sighs. No.

"Good, because we're going to have fun today." The therapist turns to Mrs Morehouse and adds, "It's time for evaluations. Why don't you come with us, and I'll show you what I have in mind."

Jason tilts his head toward me, his hand moving slyly across his book. Stupid. Speech. Woman.

I cover my mouth with my hand, so I won't laugh out loud. Jason makes her sound like a superhero: *Speech Woman! Avenger of Adverbs! Protector of Pronouns! Champion of Chitchat!*

"Bye," I mumble through my fingers.

Good-bye. He turns his page back to touch Catherine.

Reading Comprehension

1 Answer the following questions.

i Who is the narrator?

ii Why does she flinch when Jason makes a sound?

iii How does Catherine decide to draw herself?

iv What does Catherine think of the words in Jason's communication book?

v How does the speech therapist ask Jason if he is cranky? What do Catherine and Jason think about this?

vi What is Jason's opinion of his speech therapist? Why does it make Catherine laugh?

vii Who do you think "David" is?

viii Why do you think Jason dislikes his therapist?

ix Is Catherine nervous around Jason? Why or why not?

---

avenger: someone who inflicts harm in return for an injury or wrong done to oneself or another

Vocabulary

1 Complete the crossword below.

ACROSS

1. something that helps people who cannot walk to travel
3. a way of communicating using hands (4, 8)
4. a woman who helps Jason to speak (6, 9)
5. writing that visually impaired people can read

DOWN

2. what Jason uses to talk to Catherine (13, 4)

Grammar

Clauses

Clauses are groups of words that consist of a subject and a predicate. While **main clauses** form independent thoughts and can exist as complete sentences, **subordinate clauses** cannot stand alone as sentences and need to be attached to a main clause. **Relative clauses** modify a noun phrase. They too cannot exist independently and must be attached to a main clause.

Identify whether the following clauses are subordinate/dependent or relative clauses. Combine them with main clauses of your own to form complete sentences.

i that Jack had built

ii as if she was being chased by a giant spider

iii whose dog had terrorised the neighbourhood

iv although we were hungry

v whoever stole my sandwich

vi unless you promise not to tell anyone

vii while the firemen doused the flames

viii who was the best defender in the team

ix since she did not know how to swim

Writing

Write character sketches of Mrs Morehouse and Jason. Fill out the word webs below with information from the story, and base your sketches on this information.

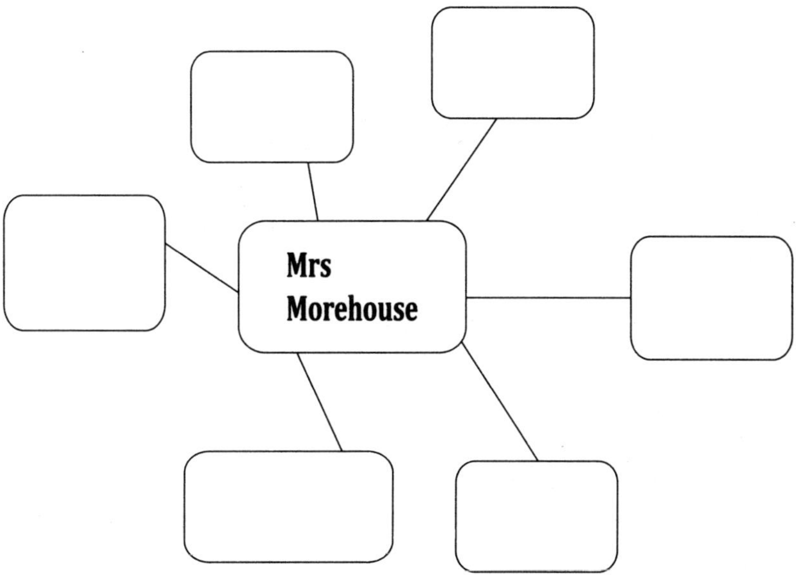

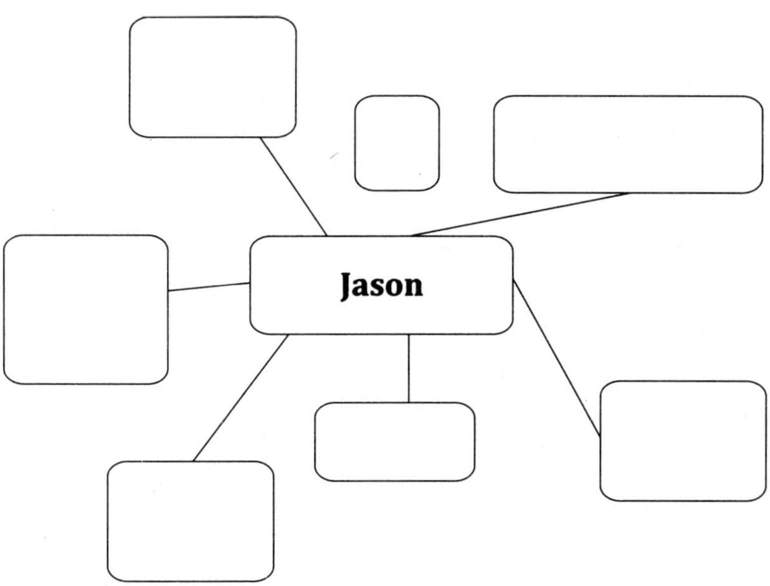

5 The Power of Hearing

***Leslee Lazar** is working towards a PhD in Neurosciences. His book* The Five Senses *is a fascinating introduction to how our senses work.*

A Bag of Gas

Among animals there are many different **auditory** systems, some of them simple and some complex. Marine animals also use sound for communication. Some, like dolphins, use high-frequency sounds that are audible to us while animals like whales use low- frequency sounds. Sharks also hear well in the range of low-frequency sounds, especially irregular sounds made by wounded or weak fish, so they can find them and eat them.

Fish have inner ears, much like ours. They are bony structures that are able to sense the vibrations; they also have receptors that have hair-like structures called cilia that convert these vibrations into electrical impulses. But as fish don't have external ears, they use their whole body to sense the vibrations in water. The vibrations travel through the body and move the bones of the inner ear, which in turn **deflect** the cilia in the inner hair cells. Like the human ear, there is a mechanism that converts this deflection into electrical signals and sends them to the fish's brain.

Some fish can hear better than others. Although they have similar inner ear mechanisms, what gives them the advantage is a bag of gas! These fish have a gas-filled sac, called gas bladder, to help them stay afloat. The pressure caused by any sound nearby can also compress the gas in the bladder. In some fishes, like carp and catfish, these gas bladders are connected to the inner ear by a series of bones. So the pulsations of the bladder caused by sound are passed on to the inner ear. This mechanism works like an amplifier and helps the fish hear

---

auditory: relating to hearing

deflect: turn aside or redirect

better. Fishes like carp and catfish have very sensitive hearing they can hear **ultrasonic** frequencies above 180000 Hz.

Lopsided Ears

Owls are born with **lopsided** ears. One of their ears is always slightly higher or lower than the other. Before we dismiss it as a freak of nature, let us look closely at its hearing abilities for a clue on why this is so.

Owls spend most of their time in the dark and have an acute sense of hearing. They can detect their prey just by hearing them move, in complete darkness. Owls have two ears, one on either side of the head, which are nothing but small slits. They also have a dish-like structure on the face, which is made up of feathers. This facial **ruff** deflects sound into the owl's ears, much like the external ear of humans does.

How does the owl know which side of its head the sound is coming from? It makes simple but very fast calculations to do this. If the sound is coming from the right side the right ear gets the sound first; if it is from the left side then the left ear gets it first. This is how many animals detect the direction of sound, but one has to keep in mind that the owl's head is small and sound from any direction will reach the nearer ear and the farther ear within a very small time interval. Let's say the interval is 200 millionth of a second. It's hard for our ears to detect such a small time difference between a sound reaching the left ear and the right, but the owl is able to do it!

The owl uses the different positions of the ear hole to find out whether the sound has come from above or below. Let's imagine that the right ear is slightly higher than eye level and the left ear is slightly

---

ultrasonic: above the frequencies of audible sound
lopsided: with one side lower or smaller than the other

ruff: collar made of ruffled fabric

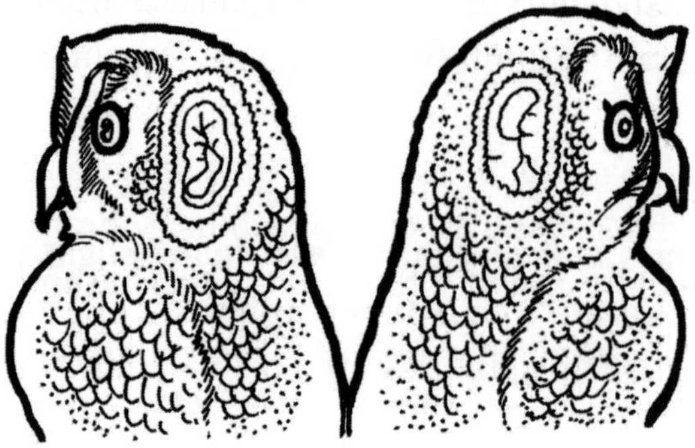

below eye level. If the sound of a prey rustling in the leaves is coming from a branch above, then the sound will reach the right ear first, since it is higher. So by knowing which ear gets the sound first, the owl can figure out whether the sound is coming from above, below, right or left!

Echoes in the Night

Bats. The very thought of these animals brings to mind vampires and dark dungeons. In reality, bats are completely harmless. They do like to hang out in dark and abandoned places but that's simply to search for their favourite food, insects. They hunt at night because that's when the insects come out to feed. People fear the sight of these animals hanging upside down in caves during the day, but they only do that because they are tired after a full night's hunting! Dracula might have given bats a bad name, but they are primarily fruit- and insect-eaters.

Bats are very good at catching their prey. They can be hired by the navy to look for enemy vessels because they use the same technology to locate their prey! They send a pulse of sound out into the environment. These sound waves hit objects and produce an echo according to the shape and distance of the object. The bats listen to the echo and are able to figure out what is present around them. The navy uses the same idea to locate enemy submarines and mines in the sea.

Bats have good vision, but since they hunt in total darkness they needed to develop some other mechanism by which to locate their prey, and hence they evolved this method, which is called echolocation.

Echolocation is not restricted to bats alone. Other mammals, like dolphins and whales and a few birds, too, have this ability. Dolphins and whales have small openings on each side of the head, but strangely, they hear with their jaws and teeth as well. They have a fat-filled cavity in the lower jaw, which is able to conduct sound vibrations in the waters that they swim in and transmit them to the middle and inner ear. In some species of whales, the jaws do the entire sound reception as their outer opening is closed shut with earwax!

Ears on the Knees

Many animals use their ears to find something to eat; but there are some organisms that use their ears to find a mate. Insects like crickets and grasshoppers expect their potential mates to sing and charm them.

Male crickets have special structures on their wings shaped like the teeth of a comb. When the wings are brought together and scraped, they produce a sound that is similar to the sound one hears when one runs a fingernail through the length of a comb. Female crickets hear these sounds and choose the best 'singer' to mate with. The twist in the tale is the location of the ear. They are located in the last place one would look for a ear on their legs, just below the 'knee'!

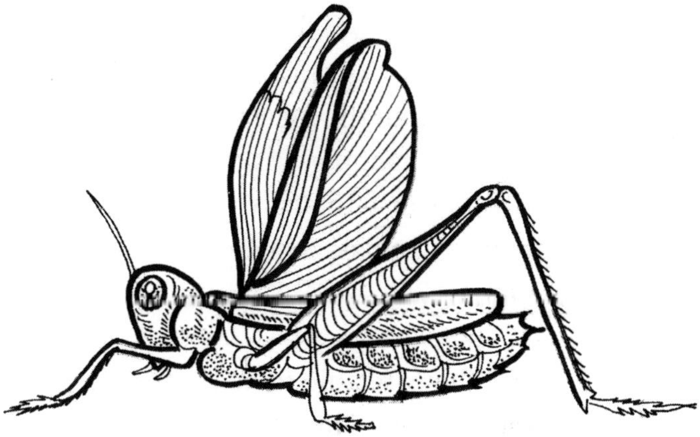

If you thought knees were a strange location for ears, then you'll find the location of grasshoppers' ears even stranger. Grasshoppers detect sound vibrations through a round **membrane** in the abdomen, located just behind the place where the hind limbs join the body.

---

membrane: a thin layer of skin or tissue

Jamming the Radar

Bats emit high-frequency sounds so that they can know the location of their prey by listening to the echo of the sound that they emitted. Insects like the praying mantis have evolved a mechanism to avoid being eaten by bats.

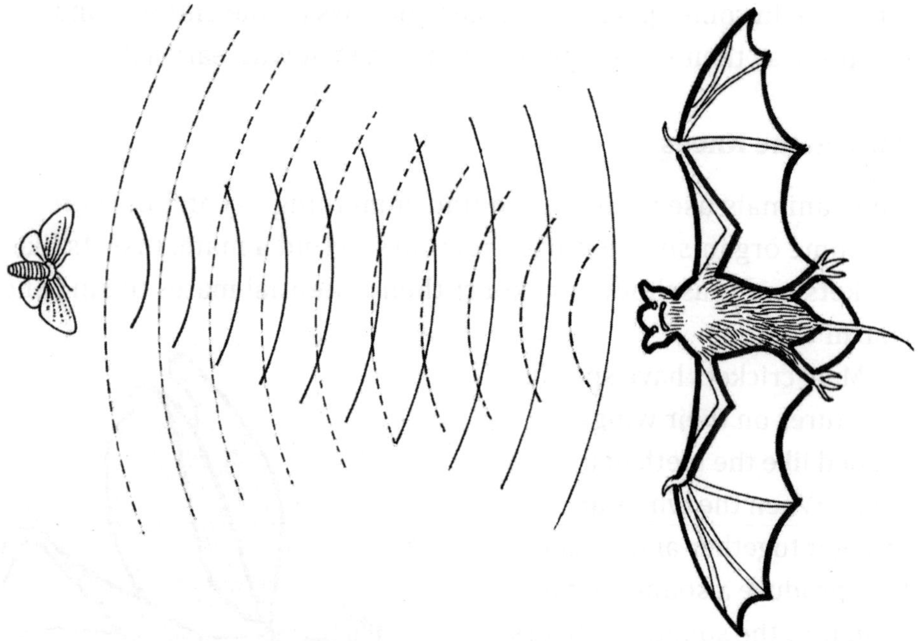

They are able to hear the high-frequency sound that bats emit to locate them. This high-frequency 'bat detector' is a single ear that is right in the middle of their body on the underside. When the bats are in hunting mode, they let out an ultrasonic sound and the praying mantis, on hearing the bat, dives abruptly towards the ground, if it is flying. This **manoeuvre** causes the bats to lose track of the insect, as bats cannot fly very close to the ground. Other insects like moths, butterflies, crickets, locusts and beetles also use this mechanism to outsmart bats.

manoeuvre: skilful movement

Reading Comprehension

1 Answer the following questions.

i What are cilia?

ii What purpose does a gas bladder serve?

iii What is the "dish-like" structure on the faces of owls? What is its function?

iv Why do you think the author feels that bats have been given a bad name?

v What similarity between the navy and bats is described by the author?

vi What is unusual about the way in which dolphins and whales experience sound?

vii Where are grasshoppers' ears?

viii How do some insects outsmart bats?

Vocabulary

1 Acronyms are abbreviations formed by the first letters of a phrase or name. People use acronyms to say something quickly. Expand the following common acronyms.

UNO ________________

SMS ________________

WHO ________________

ISRO ________________

SAARC ________________

UNESCO ________________

PETA ________________

BBC ________________

Grammar

Colons

Colons are represented by the ":" sign. They are usually used to introduce a new concept or thought. Some of the ways in which we use colons are:

(a) to introduce a list
(b) to introduce an example or explanation
(c) to introduce a question
(d) to introduce a quotation
(e) to introduce a subtitle
(f) to introduce direct speech
(g) to take the place of a conjunction

For example:

The tall man snarled at me: "Get off my land," he said.
There was only one thing for it: we'd have to go through the forest.
I remembered what Rakhi had told us: "Always carry a length of rope."
The amount of food on the table was amazing: sandwiches, cakes, pies, ice cream and a plate piled high with cookies.
There's just one thing I'd like to know: was it you who stole my pen?
His book is titled *Game of Kings: A History of Polo in India*.

1 Insert the missing colons in the following sentences.

i Their only real concern was this what would Kanika say?
ii Writing the review would be easy but for one problem I had not read the book
iii She laughed at him "You look ridiculous," she said.
iv I had made my decision it was time to confront the bullies.

v Everything in the room was white walls, ceiling, curtains, furniture, bedspread and even the floor.

vi She read out a newspaper article titled "The Cost of War How the Gulf War Damaged our Economy".

vii I have a number of things to buy for school books, notebooks, pencils, pens, a new bag and a geometry box.

Writing

Close your eyes for one minute and listen carefully to the sounds around you. Then write a paragraph describing all of the sounds you heard. What do you think caused them? Compare your paragraph with that of your partner.

Further Discussion

1 How many forms of communication can you think of? What non-traditional forms of communication are discussed in the chapters in this section?

Speaking and Listening

"Communication technology has led to a breakdown in communication". Do you think this statement is true? Organise a debate in class.

Learn More

Find out more about the following means of communication. Who uses them? How do they work?

Sonar	Braille
Morse Code	Sign Language
Whale Song	Dance and communication of bees

THE WORLD

"The wide world is all about you; you can fence yourselves in,
but you cannot forever fence it out."

—J.R.R. Tolkien

6 Two Myths about Fire

Sharada Bhanu *and* ***Padma Malini Raghavan*** *are former members of the Department of English at Stella Maris College in Chennai.*

The Titans, according to Greek **mythology**, were a race of gods sprung from the earth and sky. Prometheus was a Titan, the son of Iapetus and Asia. His name means "**forethought**" and his brother's name Epimetheus means "afterthought".

Prometheus **fashioned** the race of men out of clay. His brother had the task of distributing various qualities and abilities among the animals. Prometheus wanted to make his creation special. So he gave man technology with the help of the goddess Athena and he gave fire taken from Hephaestus. He educated man on how to use fire to work metals. In fact, the growth of civilisation depends on how skillfully man controls and uses fire.

Prometheus offered the god Zeus a sacrifice. He wanted men to have the good meat. So he made two piles of offerings. One pile had the good meat and this he covered over with the **entrails** of the animal. The second pile had all the bones and this he covered over with fat. He asked Zeus to choose and he chose the one with a lot of fat on it. On discovering the trick, Zeus was **enraged** and took away fire from man to spite Prometheus. Not to be outwitted so easily, Prometheus stole the **embers** and hid them inside a **fennel** stalk and brought it to man. (Interestingly, dry fennel makes excellent kindling and is useful to start a fire.)

Prometheus suffered a terrible punishment. He was chained to Mount Causasus in Scythia, with a stake through his middle. During the day a giant eagle ate his liver and entrails. At night, the organs

---

mythology: a set of stories or beliefs about a particular person, institution or situation, especially when exaggerated or fictitious
forethought: careful consideration of what will be necessary or may happen in the future
fashioned: made into a particular form
entrails: a person's or animal's intestines or internal organs, especially when removed or exposed
enraged: very angry; furious
embers: a small piece of burning or glowing coal or wood in a dying fire
fennel: an aromatic yellow-flowered European plant of the parsley family, with feathery leaves

grew again. The next morning the eagle was back to feed. Prometheus endured this for many centuries until Hercules came there and killed the eagle to set him free.

In Persian belief, fire is the last and most important of the creations by Ahura Mazda, the wise lord. Along with wisdom, Ahura Mazda is associated with light and brightness. His arch opponent is Ahriman or Angra Mainyu who lives in absolute darkness.

Before creation, there was emptiness and void between them. Then Ahura Mazda decided he would start his act of creation. First he created the sky, bright and shining. Then he created water pure and clear. Third on the wise lord's list was the earth, flat and round. It was flat in a very literal sense—there were no mountains or valleys. Earth had a level surface, signifying there were no inequalities. Then the wise lord created plants that were moist and sweet and supple too because of the moisture. They had no rough bark. Next came the animals, big and small. Then he created the First Man, Gayamard, handsome and bright. Now we come to the important point of our story. Sky, Water, Earth, Plants and Animals were created before Man was created. Fire was created after First Man came, to fulfil his special needs. Ahura Mazda distributed fire to all and ordered it to serve mankind both for cooking and for keeping warm.

How Angra Mainyu attacked Ahura Mazda's seven creations by bringing darkness to the sky, bitterness to water, uneven hills and valleys to the earth, thorns to the plants, thoughts of violence to animals, sickness and death to man and smoke to the fire, and how Ahura Mazda created the Seven Bounteous Immortals to protect his seven creations are part of the Zoroastrian creation story.

When a Jashan ceremony is enacted in the Zoroastrian place of worship, it is a thanksgiving for the perfect harmony in which Ahura Mazda placed his seven creations, a state we shall reclaim some day. But fire is remembered everyday as the **embodiment** of the Creator, who is radiant and luminous. It stands for spiritual light. That is why the Zoroastrian place of worship is called a Fire Temple—celebrating Ahura Mazda's special gift for man.

Reading Comprehension

1 Answer the following questions.

i What did Prometheus take from Athena and Hephaestus?

ii How did Prometheus trick Zeus?

iii What terrible punishment did Prometheus endure?

iv Who is Ahriman?

---

embodiment: the representation or expression of something in a tangible or visible form

v Why did Ahura Mazda create fire after creating the first man?
vi What is a Fire Temple? Why is it so named?
vii Why do you think fire-myths are so important to humans?

Vocabulary

1 Classify the name of gods and complete the table.
Hint: There are four gods in each column.

Odin	Sekhmet	Zeus	Minerva	Agni
Athena	Thor	Freya	Anubis	Ra
Vayu	Mercury	Aphrodite	Vulcan	Surya
Osiris	Loki	Poseidon	Mars	Indra

Greek	Roman	Hindu	Norse	Egyptian

Grammar

Modals

Modals are a special category of English language verbs. They deal with the ideas of *necessity* and *possibility*. They cannot be used as the main verb in a sentence, since they are only auxiliary (helping) verbs. Common modal verbs are: can, could, ought to, shall, may, might, must, should, will, would.
For example:
Could you tell me the time?
May I leave the room?
You **must** not leave the bathroom untidy.
The wheat crop **should** be better this year.
Modal verbs do not take **-s** in the third person. Many of them cannot be used in the past and future tenses. We use **not** to make modals negative.

1 Choose the correct modal to complete the following sentences.

i You (must have/ought to) left it in the garden.

ii (Shall/Will) we go to the park after school?

iii I wish you'd been there; you (may have/would have) really enjoyed it.

iv The poor child (must/can) be starving by now!

v We (would/ought to) give our hosts a gift for their kindness to us.

vi You (must not/cannot) forget to wear your lifejacket.

vii (Must/could) you pass the salt, please?

viii She (could/may) have to rearrange her holiday plans.

ix We (can/might) be getting a puppy soon.

x Goodbye! We (ought to/shall) all miss you!

Writing

What myths from your own culture do you think are the most important? Rewrite one such myth in your own words. Be as original as you can!

7 Yogurt and Cinnamon Dessert with Rose Geraniums and Peach

Sampurna Chattarji *is an Indian writer and translator.*

Was her name Martha, or Marsha,
the one with the **enchantress** hands?
A little eager, a little shy,
I walked into her kitchen that first morning
towards the smell of coffee and muffins.
"Blueberry!" she said, **conspiratorially**.
"Heaven," I said, one large bite
and two quick sips later. "Heaven on earth."

I counted them greedily,
three breakfasts, two dinners,
each outdoing the other.
Crisp bacon wrapped around soft seedless dates,
dips with cheese and herbs.
Served course-by-course, light pastas,
the right wine, voices **reverential** as we ate.
"*You'll* like this," she said the last evening,
knowing by then where I came from,
"It's Yogurt and Cinnamon Dessert
with Rose Geraniums and Peach."

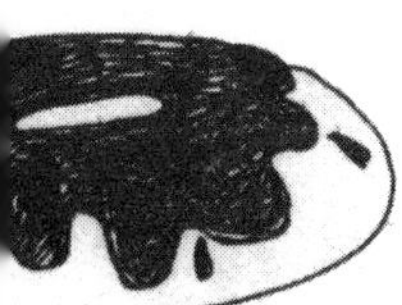

enchantress: a woman who practices magic
conspiratorially: of relating to or suggestive of a conspiracy

reverential: expressing or having a quality of reverence

I picked up a plate, and the first spoonful
Conjured up a taste I thought
I had forgotten, curd steamed with sugar
And cinnamon, a treat my mother made.
"The rose geraniums are an Irish thing,"
She said, "I picked that up in Ireland."
Her cheeks were **flushed**. Was it my delight?
Or was it the heat from her oven?
India America Ireland. Cinnamon yogurt and peach.
"You're astonishing, Martha," I said, for Martha it was,
And I was happy and close, so close, to tears.

conjured: to summon by or as if by invocation or incantation
flushed: a person's skin or face becoming red and hot typically through illness or emotion

Reading Comprehension

1 Answer the following questions.

i Who was Martha?

ii "Voices reverential as we ate." Why do you think the poet and her companions spoke in this manner?

iii How did Martha know that the poet would like the yogurt and cinnamon dessert with rose geraniums and peach?

iv What changes had Martha made to the recipe?

v "India America Ireland." How had these countries contributed to the dish?

vi Why does the poet say "for Martha it was"?

Vocabulary

1 Choose words from the box given below to complete the following phrases. Some words may be used more than once.

take	pay	have	give	make	keep
put	play	pick	do		

i to ____________ up a bad habit

ii to ____________ track of someone

iii to ____________ turns

iv to ____________ up a cause

v to ____________ a good day

vi to ____________ up with someone

vii to ____________ a compliment

viii to ____________ a decision

ix to ____________ a favour

x to ____________ a promise

xi to ____________ a secret

xii to ____________ advantage

xiii to ____________ it safe

xiv to ____________ a life

xv to ____________ advice

Writing

1 Read these two lines from the poem:

"Her cheeks were flushed. Was it my delight?"
"And I was happy and close, so close, to tears."

In these lines it is obvious that food can be a very emotional issue. Why do you think this is? Write a paragraph describing a memorable meal you have had.

8 27 Nisbat Road

***Rehan Ansari** is a journalist who has lived in New York, Lahore and Mumbai.*

The address was 27 Nisbat Road. The house no longer exists. In the nineties in Delhi, old men told me that Nisbat Road was an **elite** neighbourhood before Partition. Mr Paintal called it the Park Lane of Lahore.

How I remember it most **vividly**, from age three on, is from the tonga ride to and from the railway station to the house. This was in the early seventies. We would make a right turn at Dayal Singh College into the lane that led to the house.

There was nothing elite about the neighbourhood. Nisbat Road did not look modern, and don't underestimate the pace and height of a tonga ride for **perspective**. Modern was my school in Karachi and most things associated with the school. Karachi Grammar School had order: periods, prefects, English, even English principals, one succeeding another. KGS wasn't **chaotic** like Nisbat Road. I now know that KGS just wasn't the same kind of chaos as Nisbat Road.

If the street was non-modern, the house was really a puzzle with many pieces missing. It stood in relationship to nothing.

It was grand: a corridor long enough to play cork-ball cricket in with my cousin Nomi, with bedrooms opening to it (in each one of them Nomi and I had epic fights—the house was so spacious that until the after-effects of the fight, no adult would know), leading to a courtyard, around which were several rooms, including a huge dining room with a table that could sit ten adults.

If the house was **gargantuan**, why was the entrance severely **foreshortened**? Not only was there no room in front of the house but the lane leading to the house from Dayal Singh College on Nisbat

---

elite: a group of people considered to be superior in a particular society or organisation
vividly: producing powerful feelings or strong, clear images in the mind
perspective: the appearance of viewed objects with regard to their relative position, distance from the viewer
chaotic: in a state of complete confusion and disorder
gargantuan: enormous
foreshortened: prematurely or dramatically shortened or reduced

Road was encroached upon by new structures. The lane itself was more a drain-covering than a road. I have never come across a more **marooned** dwelling.

Whose house was it? My grandfather, an ex-civil servant, had a law practice, but this house looked like a fat *seth's* house, and not my lean grandfather's. Nana's Morris was permanently parked and he would cycle to the courts and back in his white shirt, black tie and pants.

If there was any talk of the history of the house, my grandmother would talk about another house, even grander, with stables (!) in a place called Alwar. I thought that a funny noun with a 'w' in the middle, and I did think that if it wasn't used by an old person, it would be a place on Vulcan (in the early seventies we saw *Star Trek*, in black and white, on PTV).

My grandfather would not talk at all. Every once in a while, he would disapprove of something. He didn't like us to go on the roof, which was our starship *and* our favourite solar system. The roof had many levels, like the *Enterprise*, and old store rooms full of junk, which Nomi and I pretended were destroyed planets we had beamed down upon. We dreaded that my grandfather would come home an hour or so before sunset just when kites in the old city started blossoming, and so our Mamoo (one of his sons) would feel compelled to leave the roof, and he was the one doing the flying and we happy around him.

Mamoo would fix the antenna on Friday night, so we could get a signal from Amritsar so that his sisters (my mom among them) could watch *Chitrhaar*, which was a bore. One day Nana burst out saying that it was not a good influence from there.

Except for that last phrase (there where?), he had expressed the same bad opinion about the influence of comic books, and heartily approved of my leafing through books in his drawing room library. My favourite was a *Time Magazine Map of the World* from the fifties. I badly wanted to steal that mapbook until my mother said, "Just ask him for it," and he let me borrow it. Stealing would have been preferable: less fuss.

---

marooned: trapped and alone in an inaccessible place

SHARMA STORE
27
NISBAT ROAD

His law books in the office, I only looked at in their shelves—massive and unmoveable, but I remember all of them had "India" on them, and a date: "1935".

Nobody came to meet Nana Abba, he wouldn't meet anybody either. Though he was the one who was really isolated, no one in the family had friends in the neighbourhood. We kids didn't have friends around there. The neighbourhood spoke a different language. There was no **animosity**, we just didn't have anything to do with the other families, except for the fact that we had all beamed down to the same place; they, in huge numbers, from a place called Amritsar.

My grandmother liked to go out. She would be the queen bee in the entourage of uncles, aunts and my cousins who would **convoy** down the street to a cinema on Abbott Road or Mcleod Road, and we would go to Metropole, or New Imperial (also called Moon Light), and there would be that *Star Trek* feeling about Lahore—the theatres looked **run-down**, but modern at the same time. The *Enterprise* was meant to be in the future but the technology looked dated, except that it was the opposite in Lahore: the past looked more modern than the present, as if some unreasonable "history ray" had hit Planet Lahore, and I had arrived after the event.

In 1991, finished with college, I visited Lahore, and lived there for some **stints** through the decade, writing for newspapers, working for a film studio. 27 Nisbat Road was abandoned, except by my grandmother, who lived there in the days (at nights with a daughter) hoping to attract one of her children back to it. For my mother and her siblings, Nisbat Road was the starting point for journeys that ended up either in Gulbarg, Defence, or their equivalent in Karachi, or Canadian cities of Mississauga, Oakville, Brampton and London, Ontario. But some of us among her grandchildren were interested in it.

In 1991 the old city in the evenings did not have the designated "food streets" that exist now in Gwalmandi and Purani Anarkali, or the artist Iqbal Hussain's Cookoo's Café at Taxali Gate overlooking Badshahi Mosque, the Fort and Ranjit Singh's Samadhi, nor were

---

animosity: strong hostility
convoy: to travel together as a group

run-down: in a poor or neglected state after having been prosperous
stints: a person's fixed or allotted periods of work

there the corporate and other elite organised parties in *havelis* in Lahore for *basant*. Most of the city, at dusk, had a compelling gloom. But Nomi and I, with a teenaged cousin, would go over to 27 Nisbat Road. With Nomi leading the way, usually by singing, we scared away every ghost on Nisbat Road. I say Nomi led the way because he was the only one among us who spent his teenage years in the house, and did things with abandon. He sold off Nani's furniture that lay around in various storerooms on the roof. For that terrific **exorcism** he was much **maligned** by all the parents. But in their dismay and fear, was their first collective acknowledgement of the wilfulness of the younger generation. He was our Bhagat Singh.

By the time Nani came the morning after, we had carted away our hangovers, but if I were ever to come back in the afternoon she would be sitting in the shade of the veranda on a low stool, fanning herself, making tea over a camping stove. Without signs of her children, her jewellery, her cuisine (the fish *ka saalan*), her acid wit (when I asked her for her car she said, "*pehlay tolo, phir socho, phir bolo*"—"first weigh, then think, then talk"), I'd find her sitting in a pose I never encountered her in while growing up.

Recently, I recalled her in a flash when I saw a woman in the shade of her mud house in a *basti* in Rajasthan looking out steadily for hours. This was during a trip I made to Tijara, my grandfather's birthplace.

Except for that woman's pose, nothing in that *qasba* reminded me of him or of anything in 27 Nisbat Road.

Reading Comprehension

1 Answer the following questions.

i In which city was Nisbat Road?

ii Why did the author feel that Nisbat Road was not elite?

exorcism: the expulsion or attempted expulsion of a supposed evil spirit from a person or place

maligned: spoken about in a spitefully critical manner

iii. "KGS wasn't chaotic like Nisbat Road." Comment.

iv What happened an hour before sunset?

v What was strange about the house?

vi "...it was not a good influence from there." What is the "there" the grandfather was referring to?

vii Why does the author describe Nomi as "our Bhagat Singh"?

viii Which television programmes does the author mention in the story?

Vocabulary

1 The word "urban" means something related to or belonging to a city or town. Can you guess the meanings of the following words? Look them up in the dictionary to find out whether you were right.

i urbanisation

ii suburban

iii urbane

2 The words below are all names for places where people live. Organise them according to size, from the smallest to the biggest.

i village metropolis hamlet town city megapolis

ii mansion apartment hut house cottage

iii district nation state neighbourhood city

Grammar

Gerunds

Gerunds are words that end in **-ing** and look like verbs but function as nouns within a sentence.
For example:
(a) They do not enjoy **swimming**.
(b) The choir's **singing** was terrible; they were completely out of practice.
(c) My brother received a ticket for **speeding**.

1 In the following sentences, identify whether the underlined words are verbs or gerunds.
  i My dog's only activities are eating and sleeping.
  ii Being the youngest was sometimes very useful, thought Kamala.
  iii They were playing volleyball in the park.
  iv I forgot all about paying my school fees and now they're late.
  v Bhuvan is learning to speak Russian.
  vi Seeing is believing.
  vii I always forget to pack my bag before going to bed.
  viii Just as we were about to leave it started raining.

Writing

Read the review of the movie *Spirited Away* given on the next page. The reviewer has provided a brief summary of what it is about and described some interesting aspects of the film. Write a short review of a movie you have seen. Don't forget to include the names of the director and lead actors, and to explain what you did and did not like about the movie. Try not to give away the ending!

Spirited Away
Directed by: Hayao Miyazaki

When in the process of moving to a new town, Chihiro and her parents stumble upon an entrance to the spirit world. Chihiro's parents are turned into pigs, and the ten-year-old girl finds herself alone. But a boy named Haku seems to know her and helps her get a job at the evil witch Yubaba's bath-house. It will take all of Chihiro's ingenuity and courage to free herself, her parents and her friend Haku from Yubaba's clutches and go back into the real world, and in the course of her adventure, she matures from a sullen and whiny child to a hard-working, responsible young girl.

This animated film from Japan was not only the highest-grossing film in the country when it was released way back in 2001, but also won the Academy award for best animated feature. Hayao Miyazaki is known for making films with a strong pro-environment message and *Spirited Away* is no exception. The characters, especially those from the spirit world, are sourced from Japanese mythology and folklore. The lead character was inspired by the antics of Miyazaki's friend's ten-year-old daughter, when the director wanted to come up with a character who would appeal as a role model to children.

Further Discussion

1 In "27 Nisbat Road", boys living in Lahore are influenced by American television programmes. In "Yogurt and Cinnamon Dessert with Rose Geraniums and Peach" an Indian dish picks up Irish and American influences. Do you see a similarity between these chapters? Do you think that the exchange of cultures benefits both?

2 In "Two Myths about Fire" you learnt about Greek and Zoroastrian myths. Which other cultures' myths are you familiar with? Why do you think you are more familiar with those cultures than others?

Listening and Speaking

Where is this myth? Your teacher will read out a short myth. Listen carefully and answer the following questions.

i Why did the old man put down his spear?
ii What did the old man offer the people?
iii For what purpose was the cockatoo using the fire?
iv Why did the people invite the cockatoo to a feast?
v What happened when the robin took the fire stick?
vi What reminder of his great deed does the robin carry?

Art and Culture

"We all know that Art is not truth. Art is a lie that makes us realize the truth, at least the truth that is given to us to understand."

—Pablo Picasso

9 Music

***Amy Lowell** (1874–1925) was an American poet. She won the Pulitzer poetry prize after her death.*

The neighbour sits in his window and plays the flute.
From my bed I can hear him,
And the round notes flutter and tap about the room,
And hit against each other,
Blurring to unexpected **chords**.
It is very beautiful,
With the little flute-notes all about me,
In the darkness.

chords: a term in music for a situation when three or more pitches are played at the same time or for the strings of a musical instrument

In the daytime,
The neighbour eats bread and onions with one hand
And copies music with the other.
He is fat and has a bald head,
So I do not look at him,

But run quickly past his window.
There is always the sky to look at,
Or the water in the well!
But when night comes and he plays his flute,
I think of him as a young man,
With gold **seals** hanging from his watch,
And a blue coat with silver buttons.
As I lie in my bed
The flute-notes push against my ears and lips,
And I go to sleep, dreaming.

Reading Comprehension

1 Answer the following questions.
   i At what time of the day does the neighbour play his flute?
   ii What does the neighbour look like? Why does the poet hurry past his window?
   iii How does the poet imagine the neighbour? Why does she do this?
   iv What impression of the poet do you gain from this poem?
   v "The neighbour eats bread and onions with one hand". Why do you think the poet tells us this?

---

seals: embossed emblems

Vocabulary

1 The names of fifteen musical instruments are hidden in the word grid below. Can you find them all?

I	R	A	N	T	E	F	R	A	U	C	Y	M	B	A	L	S	T	A	W
U	L	O	N	G	A	C	R	E	T	Y	N	F	A	G	R	A	G	E	R
N	E	O	L	O	G	P	R	N	O	Q	U	I	B	A	L	U	M	D	A
N	T	G	R	B	C	Y	C	E	N	B	A	L	L	G	U	T	C	U	T
T	R	T	A	D	I	M	Y	B	E	F	L	E	A	B	E	N	E	F	N
H	A	R	M	O	N	I	U	M	G	I	N	P	I	C	C	O	L	O	K
G	O	U	T	H	O	I	N	A	U	P	O	G	M	O	S	U	L	A	I
R	B	M	C	L	I	T	E	H	M	O	X	P	L	A	T	E	O	Z	T
E	O	P	J	A	I	S	P	T	M	I	Y	U	R	D	R	Y	V	I	H
A	L	E	B	E	E	U	K	U	L	E	L	E	E	T	O	L	L	Y	W
N	D	T	H	O	W	E	R	B	O	L	O	R	E	A	M	A	C	U	A
P	E	D	R	A	S	T	S	L	P	I	P	R	A	B	B	L	U	M	N
L	F	L	U	T	E	J	G	A	A	N	H	E	W	L	O	C	K	F	K
E	E	H	R	Y	N	D	U	N	D	E	O	N	M	A	N	D	O	D	C
C	C	R	A	R	T	P	I	A	N	O	N	C	A	N	E	R	A	I	V
T	R	E	P	P	I	O	T	D	T	G	E	F	O	R	T	I	S	S	D
R	I	L	A	R	G	O	A	O	I	B	A	R	C	A	R	O	L	L	A
U	J	L	O	P	W	E	R	H	K	H	D	E	I	H	A	R	P	E	R
B	S	I	T	A	R	O	N	I	C	S	J	O	P	P	A	D	S	D	O
A	L	T	I	P	O	Q	Y	S	L	A	T	E	B	I	I	T	H	E	G

10 My Last Duchess

***Robert Browning** (1812–89) was a poet and playwright from England. He was one of the most influential Victorian poets.*

That's my last duchess painted on the wall,
Looking as if she were alive. I call
That piece a wonder, now: Frà Pandolf's hands
Worked busily a day, and there she stands.
Will't please you sit and look at her? I said
"Frà Pandolf" by design, for never read
Strangers like you that pictured **countenance**,
The depth and passion of its earnest glance,
But to myself they turned (since none puts by
The curtain I have drawn for you, but I)
And seemed as they would ask me, if they durst,
How such a glance came there; so, not the first
Are you to turn and ask thus. Sir, 'twas not
Her husband's presence only, called that spot
Of joy into the Duchess' cheek: perhaps
Frà Pandolf chanced to say "Her mantle laps
Over my lady's wrist too much", or "Paint
Must never hope to reproduce the faint
Half-flush that dies along her throat": such stuff
Was courtesy, she thought, and cause enough
For calling up that spot of joy. She had
A heart how shall I say? too soon made glad,
Too easily impressed; she liked whate'er
She looked on, and her looks went everywhere.
Sir, 'twas all one! My favour at her breast,
The dropping of the daylight in the West,

---

countenance: a person's face or facial expression

The bough of cherries some **officious** fool
Broke in the orchard for her, the white mule
She rode with round the terrace all and each
Would draw from her alike the approving speech,
Or blush, at least. She thanked men, good! but thanked
Somehow, I know not how, as if she ranked
My gift of a nine-hundred-years-old name
With anybody's gift. Who'd stoop to blame
This sort of **trifling**? Even had you skill
In speech which I have not to make your will
Quite clear to such an one, and say, "Just this
Or that in you disgusts me; here you miss,
Or there exceed the mark and if she let
Herself be lessoned so, nor plainly set
Her wits to yours, **forsooth**, and make excuse,
E'en then would be some stooping; and I choose
Never to stoop. Oh sir, she smiled, no doubt,
Whene'er I passed her; but who passed without
Much the same smile? This grew; I gave commands;
Then all smiles stopped together. There she stands
As if alive. Will't please you rise? We'll meet
The company below, then. I repeat,
The Count your master's known **munificence**
Is ample warrant that no just pretense
Of mine for dowry will be disallowed;
Though his fair daughter's self, as I avowed
At starting, is my object. Nay we'll go
Together down, sir. Notice Neptune, though,
Taming a sea horse, thought a rarity,
Which Claus of Innsbruck cast in bronze for me!

officious: interfering or eager to give unwanted advice and help
trifling: of very little importance
forsooth: in truth
munificence: the quality or action of being extremely generous

Reading Comprehension

1 Answer the following questions.

i Who is speaking?

ii Who painted the portrait?

iii What simple things made the Duchess happy? Why did this make the Duke angry?

iv What was the Duke's "gift of a nine-hundred-years-old name"?

v "I choose never to stoop". Did the Duke complain to the Duchess about her behaviour?

vi Who do you think is the listener?

vii Why do you think the Duke keeps the portrait behind a curtain?

viii Why do you think the Duke is telling the listener these things?

Vocabulary

Archaic English

All languages change over time. The English we speak today is very different from the language spoken a few centuries ago. Archaic English words are words that are no longer used in everyday English but may still be read in older written works.

1 Use a dictionary to find out what the following archaic English words mean.

i ere

ii whither

iii nay

iv anon

v hark

vi mayhap

vii wherefore

viii alack

ix nigh

x sooth

xi ye

xii thee

xiii prithee

xiv verily

xv betwixt

2 Unscramble the names of these famous painters.

i tomen

ii runtre

iii gades

iv skkinnyad

v changemoille

vi ghognav

11 What is My Single Life Worth?

***Salman Rushdie** is a British-Indian writer and Booker-prize winner. Since 1989, he has been the subject of a fatwa issued by Ayatollah Ruhollah Khomeini because of his book* The Satanic Verses. *This chapter is adapted from his speech at Columbia University on 11 December 1991.*

For many people, I've **ceased** to be a human being. I've become an issue, a bother, an "affair". And has it really been so long since religions **persecuted** people, burning them as **heretics**, drowning them as witches, that you can't recognise religious persecution when you see it?

What is my single life worth? Despair whispers in my ear: "Not a lot." But I refuse to give in to despair. I know that many people do care, and are appalled by the upside-down logic of the post-fatwa world, in which a novelist can be accused of having savaged or "mugged" a whole community, becoming its **tormentor** (instead of its victim) and the **scapegoat** for its discontents (what minority is smaller and weaker than a minority of one?).

I refuse to give in to despair even though, for a thousand days and more, I've been put through a degree course in worthlessness, my own personal and specific worthlessness. My first teachers were the mobs marching down distant **boulevards**, baying for my blood, and finding, soon enough, their echoes on English streets. At first, as I watched the marchers, I felt them trampling on my heart.

"Our lives teach us who we are." I have learned the hard way that when you permit anyone else's description of reality to supplant your own—and such descriptions have been raining down on me, from

---

ceased: to have come to an end
persecuted: harassed, treated badly, especially because of one's race or political or religious beliefs
heretics: people believing in or practising religious heresy; people holding an opinion at odds with what is generally accepted

tormentor: someone who causes severe mental or physical suffering
scapegoat: a person who is blamed for the wrongdoings, mistakes or faults of others, especially for reasons of expediency
boulevards: wide streets in a town or city, typically those lined with trees

security advisers, governments, journalists, archbishops, friends, enemies, mullahs—then you might as well be dead. Obviously, a rigid, blinkered, **absolutist** world view is the easiest to keep hold of, whereas the fluid, uncertain, metamorphic picture I've always carried about is rather more vulnerable. Yet I must cling with all my might to my own soul; must hold on to its mischievous, **iconoclastic**, out-of-step clown instincts, no matter how great the storm. And if that plunges me into contradiction and **paradox**, so be it; I've lived in that messy ocean all my life. I've fished in it for my art. This turbulent sea was the sea outside my bedroom window in Bombay. It is the sea by which I was born, and which I carry within me wherever I go.

"Free speech is a **non-starter**," says one of my Islamic extremist opponents. No, sir, it is not. Free speech is the whole thing, the whole ball game. Free speech is life itself.

---

absolutist: holding absolute principles in political, philosophical or theological matters
iconoclastic: criticising or attacking cherished beliefs or institutions

paradox: a seemingly absurd or contradictory statement or proposition which when investigated may prove to be well founded or true
non-starter: a person or plan that has no chance of succeeding or being effective

Reading Comprehension

1 Answer the following questions.

i Why does the author feel that he has "ceased to be a human being" to many people?

ii What, according to the author, is the smallest minority?

iii Is the outrage against the author only coming from "mobs marching down distant boulevards"?

iv "... a rigid, blinkered, absolutist world view is the easiest to keep hold of". Do you think the author supports such a world view? How does he describe his own?

v "Free speech is a non-starter." Explain.

Vocabulary

1 Use a dictionary or thesaurus to find words in Salman Rushdie's speech given here which mean the same as the following words.

i avenue

ii bellowing

iii displace

iv uncompromising

v blinded

vi harassed

vii tumultuous

viii susceptible

Grammar

Infinitives

Infinitives usually begin with **to**, followed by the simple form of the verb. ***For example***:

to eat   to play   to read

Infinitives are not verbs—they can function as nouns, adjectives or adverbs.

1 Identify the infinitives in the following sentences.

i The boy on the burning deck had the willpower to stay.

ii You must work harder to pass.

iii The guests were ready to eat.

iv The band went to Girish's house to practice.

v Mrs Dalloway went out to buy flowers.

vi The crowds at the Natural History Museum had come to see the giant squid.

vii I forgot to record the football match last night.

Writing

Do you believe that "Free speech is a non-starter" or do you think "Free speech is the whole thing"? Write a paragraph explaining your reasoning. Remember to lay out your points in a clear, decisive manner.

Further Discussion

1 Why do you think the poem "My Last Duchess" is included in this section?

2 In the poem "Music", the poet has made certain assumptions about how musicians should look and behave. Do you have notions about how an artist looks or acts?

Listening and Speaking

Read out your favourite poem to the class. Try and read it in a natural way that is suited to the style of the poem.

Learn More

1 Below are the names of a number of famous artists. Find out when and where they lived and the forms of art for which they were famous.

Raphael	Titian
Salvador Dali	Angelica Kauffmann
Henry Moore	Frida Kahlo
Marcel Duchamp	Annie Leibovitz

2 The following are some of the books that have been banned in India. Can you find out why?

The Satanic Verses by Salman Rushdie
Unarmed Victory by Bertrand Russell
The Ramayana by Aubrey Menen
Nine Hours to Rama by Stanley Wolpert
Shivaji: Hindu King in Islamic India by James William Laine

War and Peace

"You can no more win a war than you can win an earthquake."
—Jeanette Rankin

12 The Tenth Day

***Soma Guha** was a writer and a journalist who lived in Kolkata and New Delhi. The chapter below is an extract from the second volume of her retelling of the Mahabharata,* Mahabharata: The War.

Shikhandin was at the forefront of the Pandav lines.

As Bhishma went about distributing death to the enemy troops as he had the previous day, Shikhandin kept him in constant target. But none of Shikhandin's arrows could provoke a response from Bhishma who, with a dismissive smile, carried on with his other battles.

Duhshasan came in strongly against Arjun who was creating havoc amidst the Kaurav troops. But he could not stand Arjun's power for long and soon clambered into Bhishma's chariot for shelter. Arjun kept encouraging Shikhandin to continue with his onslaught on Bhishma.

Meanwhile, Bheem was fighting Bhagadatta, Kripa, Shalya, Kritavarma, Vinda, Anuvinda, Jayadrath, Chitrasen, Vikarna, Durmarshan—a whole line-up of Kaurav warriors who had risen against him in combined attack. It was the warriors who faltered before their **formidable** foe and retreated in confusion.

When Arjun came up to join Bheem, Kaurav generals like Bhishma, Duryodhan and Brihadval tried strengthening the opposition against the duo. The battle heated up, the action was intense and ferocious.

Shikhandin had not let up on his aggression against Bhishma.

At one point, Yudhishthir thought he heard the grandsire call out his name. The two chariots were close to one another and turning his head, Yudhishthir could make out that Bhishma was indeed telling him something. With concentration, he read his great-uncle's lips.

'Where is Arjun?' the old man was saying. 'Get Arjun here.'

The time had come. Yudhishthir bounded across to his brothers and gave the word. Arjun broke away from the fight he was in and

---

formidable: hard to overcome

instantly drove to confront Bhishma. Shikhandin slipped in at the front. The Kauravs positioned themselves by the side of their commander-in-chief.

The battle that ensued rocked the skies. The earth cracked from the **vehemence** of the charging troops.

Bhishma was **indefatigable**. 'Fight to the death,' he cried, savaging through the entire Somak division of the Pandav army. Like thunder, his bowstring twanged. None but Arjun, Krishna and Shikhandin could bear the blaze of Bhishma's last battle.

Shikhandin, inspired by Arjun, deluged Bhishma with a shower of arrows. But it seemed from the way he continued to resist Arjun and ravage the Pandav troops that the Kaurav commander could not care less. Duhshasan was admirable in his valiant defence of Bhishma. All except Arjun had to retreat, unable to beat the stout defender.

Without a break, Arjun discharged his arrows and brought ruin upon his cowering foes. There seemed to be no escape from the Gandeev's rain of fire. Duryodhan, himself fighting valiantly, provided reinforcement after reinforcement but there was no stemming the force of Arjun. Kripa, Shalya, Duhshasan, Vikarna, Vimshati all had to withdraw eventually.

Only Bhishma fought on like a roaring lion. Alone, he destroyed no less than ten thousand men on elephants, fourteen thousand foot soldiers, ten thousand horsemen, one thousand elephants, and seven superbly skilled warriors of the Pandav army. Virat suffered another **bereavement** in the death of his brother Shatanik.

'Arjun, kill Bhishma right now,' said Krishna.

But it was easier said than done. The shroud of arrows conjured up by Arjun was instantly shredded by Bhishma. Then Arjun had to rescue Bheem, Dhrishtadyumna, Abhimanyu, Satyaki, Ghatotkach and others from Bhishma's aggression.

Shikhandin, aided by Arjun, kept up his relentless attack. Satyaki, Chekitan, Dhrishtadyumna, Virat, Drupad, Nakul, Sahadev, Abhimanyu and Draupadi's sons involved Bhishma in **intermittent** battles.

---

vehemence: intensity of expression
indefatigable: seeming to be incapable of tiring

bereavement: loss, particularly due to death
intermittent: stopping and starting at irregular intervals

An arrow from Arjun cut Bhishma's bow in two. That instigated Drona, Kritavarma, Jayadrath, Bhurishravas, Shal, Shalya and Bhagadatta into leading a fresh charge against Arjun. Satyaki, Bheem, Dhrishtadyumna, Virat and Abhimanyu immediately rose to the Pandav's defence.

Shikhandin increased the pace of his assault. He could feel the presence of Arjun right behind. An arrow shot out and smoothly halved another of Bhishma's bows. The Kaurav commander hurled a missile in Arjun's direction. The Pandav destroyed it forthwith.

'Yes,' Bhishma told himself. 'Yes, I can die now.'

A flash lit up the firmament. A wind tore through the battlefield of Kurukshetra. Faces formed in heaven. 'Yes,' they whispered. 'Yes, the end of the curse is nigh.'

Arjun steeled himself, his eyes seeking out the weak spots in Bhishma's armour. Bhishma stood tall in his chariot, rock-still, unmoving. Shikhandin, in between, rose like the **avenging** past.

The arrows came in a thick torrent straight at the waiting warrior. At first they glanced past the iron armour, at first they had little effect ... but then, the arrows grew grim, they turned in with weird, bizarre tongues and started to scathe the heart.

'Ah, Duhshasan,' said Bhishma, to the warrior fighting by his side, 'these are not Shikhandin's arrows. These must come from Arjun, for they **char** my flesh as young crabs tear their mother's body.'

Bhishma took up a missile and threw it with force at his worthy opponent. Arjun, with three arrows, cut the weapon into pieces even as it speeded through the air. Bhishma geared up with his sword and shield. But even before he could get to the ground to battle it out on foot, a missile from Arjun broke the sword to fragments and scattered the shield in shreds.

The holes in the armour grew, the gashes showed up large, yet Bhishma kept fighting to the last of his strength. As the flowing blood mingled with the saffron rays of the setting sun, the father of the Kaurav clan fell from his chariot.

All movement ceased.

---

avenging: taking revenge
char: burn or scorch

The Fallen Warrior

Bhishma rested on a bed of arrows. Pierced with shafts from shoulder to toe, his body never touched the ground. It was the final honour for a great hero.

The gods looked down and said, 'O brave warrior! O great soul! The sun is in the south. Why should you die now?'

I have not died yet, thought Bhishma.

Wild geese were on their flight. 'The sun is in the south,' they seemed to cry. 'Will you die now?'

'No,' Bhishma whispered. 'Only when the sun is in the north ...'

The sky was blue and soft in welcome. The earth was damp with tears. The breeze blew gently. The world is at peace, thought Bhishma.

Just then he woke up to the sound of converging footsteps. His head had fallen back. His vision swam.

'Lift my head,' he murmured. 'Give it support.'

Duryodhan rushed up with cushions as soft as feather.

'That's not my pillow.' whispered Bhishma with the shadow of a smile. 'Arjun, my son, give me my pillow.'

The warriors surrounding Bhishma stood aside to let Arjun come up. With hollow eyes, the prince came and stood in front of the dying man.

'Grand-uncle,' he whispered brokenly.

'Arjun, give me my pillow,' Bhishma repeated.

Touching the feet of his grandsire, Arjun placed three arrows right under Bhishma's head to lift and support it. 'Look, how clever my boy is,' Bhishma said.

When Duryodhan brought in the best of physicians to attend to the injuries, Bhishma dismissed them. 'Of what use is medicine to me now?' he said.

He slowly moved his tongue over his bloodless lips. Then, he added, 'But I am thirsty. My mouth is dry. Get me a drink.'

Expensive wine and rose-scented water were brought immediately. But the venerable warrior grimaced.

'Arjun,' he called 'You have given me a bed and a pillow. Now let me have a drink.'

Arjun moved some distance away and then aiming his shaft, struck at a patch of ground to the right of the fallen warrior. The shaft went deep into the earth and out spurted a fountain of crystal-clear water to fall straight into the open mouth of Bhishma. It was as if Ganga herself had risen to quench the thirst of her son.

Bhishma gulped greedily.

Satiated, he blessed Arjun a thousand times. 'You are Arjun, the supreme warrior,' he said. 'Yours is the victory.'

Then Bhishma spoke to Duryodhan. 'Did you see Arjun sate my thirst? Can anyone match up to him? Let my end usher in the end to your violence. Make peace with your cousins. Don't hasten your own doom.'

But Duryodhan would not meet the grandsire's eyes. He stood wordlessly, obstinacy stiffening his spine. The sky was dark.

Bhishma gave a sigh. 'I will lie here,' he said. 'Only when the sun is in the north, shall I take my leave. Those of you who are alive then may come and bid me farewell.'

Moonlight etched out the **silhouette**s of warriors returning to camp.

Under a dome of stars, Bhishma closed his eyes.

Night

The night was at its thickest when Bhishma looked up. Moonlight fell strong on his face. The torchlights marking out his space sent out pale flickers. The guards stood by in silence.

Bhishma felt a touch on his feet. He felt a drop of water.

'Who is it?' he called out weakly.

No one replied.

'Who is it?' Bhishma called out again.

A shape emerged before him. 'I am Radheya, the sore in your eyes, the bane of your life.'

---

silhouette: outline

Karna! Bhishma made a dismissive gesture to the guards. The sentry withdrew.

'Come here, my boy,' the old man said, 'come by my side.'

When Karna drew near, Bhishma could see that he had been crying. The grandsire extended an arm and gathered the mournful visitor close. Like a son, Karna fitted into the father's embrace.

'It's good of you to come,' said Bhishma. 'You are not Radheya. You are not a charioteer's son. I know you are the son of Surya. You are Kunti's firstborn. Vyas, the seer, told me all. I have not hated you, Karna. I only wanted to change your arrogance, your attitude towards the Pandavs. You have always envied men of true merit, but you are not really at fault. It is your unusual birth that has led you to it and the unholy company of your young patron. These are the reasons why I abused you so many times in the court.'

Bhishma smiled gently at Karna and tightened the arm around him.

'I know what you are capable of,' the grandsire said. 'Few among the gods can match your power. I have seen your courage and your generosity. But as the guiding father of this enormous clan, I could not praise you openly. I would have been misunderstood by the Pandavs, and by the Kauravs too. The rift would have widened even faster. But trust me, I have known your strength all along. You stand equal to Arjun and Krishna in skill of weapons. You would do well to lend support to the Pandavs. They are your brothers. Make peace with them. They are your brothers.'

After a thoughtful pause, Karna spoke. 'Grandfather,' he said, 'I know I am Kunti's son. But I have tasted Duryodhan's salt and have to repay the debt I owe to him, even if with my life. I must be true to him, to be true to myself. Duryodhan has given me his love and trust, I cannot fail him now. I have made a lot of mistakes. But this once, you must see I am right ...'

'Yes, you are right,' said Bhishma with a sigh. 'Go forth to the battlefield then and fight like a true warrior.'

Karna, with tears in his eyes, begged forgiveness of the dying man.

'I was ignorant,' he said, 'I have wronged you deeply in word and deed.'

Bhishma placed his palm on the tormented head and blessed him from the heart.

Karna made his way back to camp, in the pink haze of a new sunrise.

Strategy

When Karna in battlegear stood amidst the Kaurav troops, their joy knew no bounds. 'Karna, you are our leader now,' they said, greeting him with warmth and respect. There was **jubilation** among the generals too.

'Bhishma wouldn't kill the Pandavs, out of affection, but it's a different story with Karna,' they said to each other. 'The Pandavs cannot hope to escape from Karna's arrows. Victory is within our grasp.'

But Karna seemed to be deep in thought. With determined steps, he moved towards Duryodhan's tent and stepped inside. Duryodhan too was looking thoughtful. As Karna entered, the Kaurav prince got up to his feet and smiled.

'Am I greeting our new commander-in-chief then?' Duryodhan asked.

Karna did not say anything.

'All our men want you to lead them in battle, Karna,' Duryodhan spoke again. 'No doubt you are the best candidate to fill Bhishma's place. Well, what do you say?'

'Any one of the warrior-kings fighting for you could lead the army,' said Karna. 'They are all equally strong, greatly skilled, courageous and intelligent. But to pick one of them as commander-in-chief would offend the others. They might hold back in battle, and this would weaken the morale of the army. Only Dronacharya stands beyond all competition. He is the **mentor** of all warriors, the master of arms. If you'll take my advice, make Drona the commander-in-chief of your army.'

Duryodhan nodded in agreement. He looked rather relieved.

Drona was happy to accept the position. He had been expecting it.

'I shall do my best for you,' he told Duryodhan.

The generals sat down for a conference.

---

jubilation: rejoicing
mentor: a trusted guide or teacher

'What we are setting out to do is to capture Yudhishthir alive,' began Duryodhan, looking at Drona. 'Never mind winning the war. Just get me Yudhishthir alive and your job will be done.'

Drona was surprised, to say the least. And pleased. So Duryodhan still has some humane qualities left in him, he thought. Or like most people, perhaps he too has finally fallen under the spell of Yudhishthir's greatness. To let off the Pandavs so lightly! Has Duryodhan developed a soft corner for his cousins at last? Did Bhishma's end have such an effect on him? Whatever the reason, it had worked out for the best. Drona thanked the gods.

But he had rejoiced too soon. For Duryodhan explained his strategy further.

'We stand to gain nothing by killing Yudhishthir,' he said. 'It would fan Arjun's rage even further. The war will turn dangerous as never before. And if it ends with the destruction of both the armies, Krishna will still be alive to place Kunti or Draupadi on the sovereign's throne. So what do we gain? Nothing. Therefore, it's my plan to play on Yudhishthir's **naiveté** once again. Get him alive, make him gamble and turn them out to the forests for another twelve years. Success—at no further cost to ourselves. The last ten days have been a nightmare.'

Drona's hopes plunged. What a fool he was to have imagined that Duryodhan could change his colours! But still, Drona thought with a slight smile, Yudhishthir is free of the death sentence.

'I shall fight to the last to fulfil your wish,' Drona gave his word to Duryodhan. 'Yudhishthir will be your prisoner.'

To the loud acclaim of his army, the new commander-in-chief took his position in the Kaurav frontline.

Reading Comprehension

1 Why did Duhshasan clamber into Bhishma's chariot?
2. What did Yudhishthir hear? What message did Bhishma convey to him?

---

naiveté: lack of sophistication

3. How many men and animals did Bhishma destroy?
4. What happened after Bhishma's bow was cut in two?
5. How did Bhishma know that the arrows had come from Arjun and not Shikhandin?
6. After his fall, what two things did Bhishma ask for? How did Arjun provide these things?
7. What advice did Bhishma give to Karna? What was Karna's reply?
8. Who was chosen as the commander-in-chief of the army? What reason did Karna give for this?
9. Why didn't Duryodhan wish to kill Yudhishthir?
10. Bhishma was fighting in Duryodhan's army. Do you think he preferred Duryodhan to Arjun? Give reasons for your answer.

Vocabulary

1 Many of the expressions we use in day-to-day life are derived from the language of war. In the sentences below, find and underline the war-related words and phrases. Find out what they originally meant. What do they mean in the context of these sentences?

- i The environmentalist group launched a campaign to raise awareness about global warming.
- ii After arguing for hours we finally declared a truce.
- iii At the press conference after the match, the two players were bombarded with questions.
- iv Each of us thought that the other would catch the ball and it fell harmlessly into the no-man's-land between us.
- v His much-hyped new movie turned out to be a dud.
- vi With his new prize-winning novel, Misra joins the ranks of India's most distinguished writers and thinkers.
- vii We all told her that it was a bad idea but she stuck to her guns and went ahead with it anyway.

viii My sister and I joined forces to convince our parents to let us get a puppy.

Grammar

Gerunds and Infinitives

1 Fill in each blank with either an infinitive or a gerund based on the word given in brackets. Remember that in some cases either an infinitive or a gerund may be correct.

i I plan __________ (visit) my grandparents on Tuesday.

ii She practiced __________ (dribble) on the basketball courts.

iii I love __________ (sleep) outdoors.

iv I plan to try __________ (run) the marathon next year.

v He has decided __________ (accept) the offer of a job in Mumbai.

vi The politicians all voted against __________ (amend) the law.

vii The dogs came __________ (run) to greet my father.

viii He promised __________ (buy) presents for everyone.

ix Did you remember __________ (turn) off the lights?

x Try __________ (eat) something; it'll make you feel better.

xi The speaker paused .... (take) a sip of water.

xii I stopped .... (play) hockey after my third ankle injury.

Writing

A book review should give the reader an idea of what the book is like and what are its good and bad points without giving too much away. Read the review of *The Count of Monte Cristo*. Write a similar review of your favourite book.

The Count of Monte Cristo
Written by: Alexandre Dumas

This is a story of jealousy, riches and retribution set in 19th century France. A young sailor named Edmond Dantes is falsely accused by three people of plotting to overthrow the king of France. He is arrested on the day he is supposed to marry his fiancée Mercedes, and is unjustly sentenced to life imprisonment in the dreaded island of Chateau d'lf. Edmond, in the course of 14 years of confinement, makes friends with a fellow-prisoner named Father Faria who tells him of an island full of treasure. Edmond manages to escape his prison, and using the wealth from the island, he plots revenge against the three men who destroyed his life.

One of the most famous adventure stories of all time, Dumas expertly mixes real historical and political characters and incidents with his fictional cast of characters. But the themes of *The Count of Monte Cristo* — justice, vengeance and mercy — are universal, and make the book a beloved classic for all ages despite its formidable page-length. It has also served as the inspiration for a number of films and plays, and even an animated series.

13 The Battle of Blenheim

Robert Southey *(1774–1843) was an English Romantic poet. He is also known as a writer of biographies. In addition, it was in one of his books that the story of Goldilocks and the Three Bears first appeared. The poem below is one of the earliest anti-war poems.*

It was a summer evening,
Old Kaspar's work was done,
And he before his cottage door
Was sitting in the sun,
And by him sported on the green
His little grandchild Wilhelmine.

She saw her brother Peterkin
Roll something large and round
Which he beside the **rivulet**
In playing there had found;
He came to ask what he had found,
That was so large, and smooth, and round.

Old Kaspar took it from the boy,
Who stood expectant by;
And then the old man shook his head,
And with a natural sigh,
"'Tis some poor fellow's skull," said he,
"Who fell in the great victory."

"I find them in the garden,
For there's many here about;
And often when I go to plough,

rivulet: a small stream of water

The **ploughshare** turns them out!
For many thousand men," said he,
"Were slain in that great victory."

"Now tell us what 'twas all about,"
Young Peterkin, he cries;
And little Wilhelmine looks up
With wonder-waiting eyes;
"Now tell us all about the war,
And what they fought each other for."

"It was the English," Kaspar cried,
"Who put the French to **rout**;
But what they fought each other for
I could not well make out;
But everybody said," quoth he,
"That 'twas a famous victory."

My father lived at Blenheim then,
Yon little stream hard by;
They burnt his dwelling to the ground,
And he was forced to fly;
So with his wife and child he fled,
Nor had he where to rest his head.

With fire and sword the country round
Was wasted far and wide,
And many a childing mother then,
And new-born baby died;
But things like that, you know, must be
At every famous victory.

They said it was a shocking sight
After the field was won;

ploughshare: the main cutting blade of a plough, behind the coulter

rout: a decisive defeat

For many thousand bodies here
Lay rotting in the sun;
But things like that, you know, must be
After a famous victory.

"Great praise the Duke of Marlbro' won,
And our good Prince Eugene."
"Why, 'twas a very wicked thing!"
Said little Wilhelmine.
"Nay ... nay ... my little girl," quoth he,
"It was a famous victory."

"And everybody praised the Duke
Who this great fight did win."
"But what good came of it at last?"
Quoth little Peterkin.
"Why, that I cannot tell," said he,
"But 'twas a famous victory."

Reading Comprehension

1 Answer the following questions.
   - i Who were Peterkin and Wilhelmine?
   - ii What had Peterkin found?
   - iii What had happened to Kaspar's father?
   - iv According to Kaspar, what was the reason for the war?
   - v What results of the war did Kaspar mention?
   - vi What did Wilhelmine think of the war? Why do you think she felt this way?
   - vii Did the war have a positive outcome?
   - viii Wilhelmine describes the war as "a very wicked thing" while Kaspar believes it was "a famous victory". Who do you think the poet agrees with? Give reasons for your answer.

Vocabulary

B	M	I
L		E
E	N	H

How many words can you make from the letters above?

Writing

What does the poem tell us about Kaspar's character? Describe him in a short paragraph.

Further Discussion

1 In the poem "The Battle of Blenheim" the children keep asking what the war was about. Do you think that the reasons for the fighting are clear in either of the chapters in this section?

2 In "The Battle of Blenheim" war is portrayed as meaningless destruction. Do you think that the chapter "The Tenth Day" also depicts this view of war? Why or why not?

Speaking and Listening

Read the following lines from Tennyson's poem "The Charge of the Light Brigade" out loud. How do you think the poet invokes the feeling that a war is taking place?

Flash'd all their sabres bare,
Flash'd as they turned in air
Sabring the gunners there,
Charging an army while
All the world wonder'd:
Plunged in the battery-smoke
Right thro' the line they broke;
Cossack and Russian
Reel'd from the sabre-stroke
Shatter'd and sunder'd.
Then they rode back, but not
Not the six hundred.

Learn More

The Battle of Blenheim is also known as the Second Battle of Höchstädt. It was fought in 1704. It was part of the War of the Spanish Succession, which was fought between a number of European countries. Use your library or the internet to learn more about the reasons for the War of the Spanish Succession.

MYSTERIES

"Without mysteries, life would be very dull indeed. What would be left to strive for if everything were known?"

—Charles de Lint

14 The Purloined Letter

***Edgar Allan Poe** (1809–49) was an American writer of horror, science fiction and mystery stories. His character Dupin is one of the earliest detectives in literature and was one of the major inspirations behind the character of Sherlock Holmes.*

CHARACTERS:

DUPIN, a private detective in Paris

EDGAR, Dupin's friend

PREFECT OF POLICE, the head of the Paris police force

KING, the ruler of France

QUEEN, the King's young wife

MINISTER D, a scoundrel who works for the King

NARRATOR (Edgar)

[Note: The Narrator and Edgar are the same character, but should be played by different actors.]

Scene One

NARRATOR: Just after dark one gusty autumn evening, I was enjoying a visit with my friend, Auguste Dupin. As we sat in silence, the door was thrown open and in came our old acquaintance, the Prefect of the police.

DUPIN (*standing*): Greetings, my friend! Have a seat while I light the lamps. To what do we owe the honour of this visit?

---

gusty: blowing in gusts

PREFECT: I have come to ask your opinion on something, Dupin. It's official business that is causing me a great deal of trouble.

DUPIN (*sitting*): Ah! If it is anything requiring thought, we should discuss it while sitting in the dark.

PREFECT (*chuckling*): Now, there's another one of your old notions!

NARRATOR: The Prefect called everything "odd" that was beyond his own comprehension. He lived in a world full of "oddities".

EDGAR: What is the difficulty now? A murder?

PREFECT: Oh no, nothing like that. The mystery is very simple indeed. I don't doubt that we can solve it ourselves. But then I thought Dupin would like to hear the details of the case, because it is so ... odd. We have been puzzled because the mystery is so simple, yet it has us baffled.

DUPIN: Perhaps it is the simplicity of the case which baffles you.

PREFECT (*laughing*): What nonsense!

EDGAR: And what are the facts of this mystery?

PREFECT: I will tell you. But let me caution you that this case demands the greatest secrecy. I would lose my job if anyone found out I told you about the case. Well then, here are the facts ...

Scene Two

NARRATOR: The Prefect told us his story. It started a few months before, when the Queen of France received a letter. She was reading it when the King entered.

KING: My dear, what is that you are reading?

QUEEN (*startled*): This? Oh, it is nothing! (*She obviously does not want the King to see the letter.*)

NARRATOR: The Queen began to hide the letter in a drawer, then decided it best to simply toss it onto her desk, so as not to arouse suspicion. At that instant, Minster D entered the room.

MINISTER D (*bowing*): Your majesties, thank you for seeing me. I have a few matters of business to discuss.

KING: You may proceed.

MINISTER D: Thank you. But, her majesty the Queen seems nervous.

QUEEN (*eyeing the letter*): Oh, it is nothing.

MINISTER D (*following her glance*): I see.

NARRATOR: Minister D, being a bold scoundrel, immediately saw that the Queen wished to hide the letter from the King. He placed a letter he had brought with him onto the desk next to the Queen's letter, then began discussing business. After fifteen minutes or so, he deliberately picked up the Queen's letter, leaving his own.

QUEEN (*gasping*): No!

KING: What is it, dear?

QUEEN: Oh... er... nothing.

MINISTER D (*smiling with* ***malice***): Very good. I will leave you now. (*Bowing to the King*) Good day, your majesty. (*Bowing to the Queen*). Your highness, I'm sure we will talk soon.

Scene Three

EDGAR: So it's blackmail!

PREFECT: Exactly. Minster D has the letter. He threatens to give it to the King, unless the Queen does just as he asks. Minister D has used his power to gain political advantage. The Queen is desperate to get the letter back, and has given the job to me.

---

malice: the desire to harm someone; ill-will

EDGAR: Is it certain that Minister D still has the letter?

PREFECT: He must. For his blackmail to work, he must be in a position to show the King the letter immediately. If he had already done so, I am sure that all of Paris would know!

EDGAR: But you have done this sort of thing often before.

PREFECT: Oh, yes. And for this reason I had great hopes. Minister D is seldom home at night. I have keys, as you know, which can open any room or cabinet in Paris. For the past three months we have been busy **ransacking** Minister D's apartment. To no avail—we have not found the letter.

EDGAR: Is it possible that Minister D is carrying the letter with him?

PREFECT: No. Three times I have had patrolmen **waylay** Minister D and search him. He did not have the letter with him.

DUPIN: You could have spared yourself the trouble. The Minister is not altogether a fool, but then he's a poet, which is almost the same thing.

EDGAR: Did you search Minister D's apartment thoroughly?

PREFECT: Of course! We took our time and searched everywhere. We opened every possible drawer ...

EDGAR: How about secret drawers?

PREFECT: There is no such thing to the trained eye. We probed the furniture cushions with long needles. We carefully took apart the tables and chairs—

EDGAR: Why on earth did you do that?

PREFECT: A letter could be hidden in a hollow leg or under the top of a table or seat of a chair.

DUPIN: Was this letter hidden in that fashion?

PREFECT: No. We put the furniture back together. Then we looked

---

ransacking: going through (a place) stealing things and causing damage

waylay: stop or interrupt (someone) and detain them in conversation or trouble them in some other way behind mirrors and pictures, in the mattress and bedclothes, behind curtains and under carpets. We examined every square inch with a microscope, searching for a secret compartment. Then we searched the houses on either side of Minster D's house.

EDGAR: The two other houses! You have had a great deal of trouble!

PREFECT (*blushing*): Yes. But her majesty has offered a substantial reward.

EDGAR: Reward or no, you have not found the letter. You must be mistaken in thinking Minister D has it in his rooms.

PREFECT: I am afraid you're right. Dupin, what do you think I should do?

DUPIN: Keep looking.

PREFECT: Is that the best advice you can give?

DUPIN (*shrugging his shoulders*): As you said, the letter must be somewhere close at hand. You simply haven't found it yet. Do you have a description of the letter?

PREFECT (*sighing*): Yes, I do.

NARRATOR: The Prefect took out a notebook and proceeded to read a detailed description of the missing document. After he finished reading the description, he left, more depressed than I had ever seen him before.

Scene Four

NARRATOR: About a month later, the Prefect paid us another visit.

EDGAR: Well, Prefect, what about the **purloined** letter? Did you find it?

PREFECT: No, confound it, although I followed Dupin's advice and searched Minister D's rooms again. It was wasted time, as I knew it would be.

---

purloined: stolen

DUPIN: How much was the reward offered, did you say?

PREFECT: It's big enough that I would gladly write a cheque in the amount of 50,000 francs to anyone who could give me the letter.

DUPIN: In that case, get out your chequebook. I will give you the letter.

NARRATOR: I was astounded. The Prefect was absolutely **thunderstruck**. He stared silently at my friend, and then took out his chequebook, wrote a cheque for 50,000 francs, and handed it to Dupin. My friend studied it carefully for a moment, slipped it into his pocketbook, then unlocked his desk drawer. He took out a letter and handed it to the Prefect.

PREFECT (*his eyes popping out*): But ... but ... how?!

NARRATOR: Then, without another word, the Prefect rushed out of our rooms with the letter.

DUPIN: The police are very able ... in their way. Unfortunately, they are no brighter or stupider than the common mass of people. Their investigations often fail when they encounter a criminal smarter than they are—and often when they deal with criminals who are not as smart.

EDGAR: But they conducted a thorough search!

DUPIN: Of course. But they searched in places where they themselves might have hidden the letter! They did not think that Minister D, who is no fool, would **anticipate** that his rooms would be searched. Of course, he would never hide the letter behind a mirror, or in a hollow table leg, because if he did it would certainly be found. He would choose a simpler place to hide it. In fact, he would choose not to hide it at all!

EDGAR: I think I understand your reasoning. But how did you manage to get hold of the letter?

DUPIN: It was simple. I took it!

thunderstruck: extremely surprised or shocked

anticipate: regard as probable; expect or predict

Scene Five

NARRATOR: Dupin told me how he paid a visit to Minister D himself.

MINISTER D (*yawning*): Why, hello, Dupin. What brings you to my rooms?

DUPIN: I was in the neighbourhood and thought I would stop in for a chat.

MINISTER D: It is good to see you. But why are you wearing dark glasses?

DUPIN: My eyes are tired and the light bothers them.

NARRATOR: Dupin actually wore the glasses so that his eyes could wander around the room without Minister D suspecting. They soon fell on a cheap card rack which dangled from a dirty blue ribbon beneath the fireplace mantel. In the rack, plain to see, was a letter. Unlike the purloined letter, it was dirty and crumpled, with a woman's handwriting on the outside. Dupin stayed for a while, chatting with the minister.

DUPIN: Thank you for seeing me, sir. I have enjoyed our chat.

MINISTER D: So have I. Please feel free to call again.

NARRATOR: Dupin left the room.

MINISTER D: Dupin! Wait! (*Dupin is gone.*) The fool. He left his snuff box behind!

Scene Six

NARRATOR: The next day, Dupin returned to the rooms of Minister D.

DUPIN: I'm sorry to trouble you, my friend. I forgot something yesterday.

MINISTER D: Your snuff box. Here it is—what is that?!

NARRATOR: A sound like gunfire cracked through the air, followed by screams. Minister D rushed to the window. As Minister D looked out the window, Dupin walked over to the mantle, took the ragged letter from the rack, and replaced it with a duplicate he had made.

MINISTER D (*turning from the window*): Some prankster burst a balloon. Well Dupin, will you stay to chat?

DUPIN: I am afraid not, my friend. I have what I came for!

Scene Seven

NARRATOR: Dupin smiled with satisfaction as he told me his story.

DUPIN: Of course, the "prankster" with the balloon was an agent I had hired to distract the minister.

EDGAR: But the letter you took looked nothing like the Queen's letter. Hers was neat and addressed in a man's hand. The letter in the rack was ragged, covered with dirt, and addressed by a woman.

DUPIN: Of course. It was so unlike the Queen's letter—in every detail—that I knew it must be a fake. When I got it back here, I found the Queen's letter wrapped up inside the false letter.

EDGAR: Does Minister D know he has been had?

DUPIN: I doubt it. The copy I made of his letter is perfect. He has no reason to open it up—not until the Queen defies him. When that happens, he is in for a rude surprise.

EDGAR: Oh, yes? What did you say in the letter you left?

DUPIN: Oh, just a personal message. Something along the lines that scoundrels can hide in plain sight—but not forever.

Reading Comprehension

1 Answer the following questions.

   i Why had the Prefect come to visit Dupin?
   ii How had Minister D managed to take the Queen's letter?
   iii Why had the police taken apart Minister D's furniture?
   iv How did Dupin reason that Minister D had not hidden the letter?
   v Why did Dupin leave his snuff box at Minister D's house?
   vi How had Dupin known that the letter was a fake?
   vii "The Prefect called everything 'odd' that was beyond his own comprehension. He lived in a world full of 'oddities'". What is the narrator's opinion of the Prefect?

Vocabulary

1 C. Auguste Dupin is a famous fictional detective created by Edgar Allan Poe. Do you know the names of the creators of these other famous fictional detectives? The first has been done for you.

   i Sherlock Holmes: <u>Sir Arthur Conan Doyle</u>

   ii Nancy Drew: ____________________

   iii Byomkesh Bakshi: ____________________

   iv Frederick Algernon Trotteville: ____________________

   v Precious Ramotswe: ____________________

   vi Arsene Lupin: ____________________

   vii Inspector Clouseau: ____________________

viii Feluda: ____________________

ix Father Brown: ____________________

x Miss Marple: ____________________

xi Lord Peter Wimsey: ____________________

xii Jupiter Jones: ____________________

Writing

Write an informal letter to a friend inviting him or her to come and visit you during the winter holidays.

15 The Secret

Katherine Mansfield *(1888-1923) was a Modernist author who was born and brought up in New Zealand. She lived in England from 1908. She is best known for her short stories, particularly "The Garden Party", "The Doll's House" and "The Fly". Mansfield died of tuberculosis at the age of thirty-four.*

In the profoundest ocean
There is a rainbow shell,
It is always there, shining most stilly
Under the greatest storm waves
That the old Greek called "ripples of laughter."
As you listen, the rainbow shell
Sings—in the **profoundest** ocean.
It is always there, singing most silently!

profoundest: with the greatest intensity

Reading Comprehension

1 Answer the following questions.

i How do you think the shell sings?

ii Is the shell affected by the "greatest storm waves"?

iii What are described as "ripples of laughter"?

iv Why do you think the shell is described as a "rainbow shell"?

Vocabulary

Alliteration

Alliteration is a way of writing in which words with the same consonant sounds (usually at the beginning of the word) are brought together. The first letters of the words need not be the same. ***For example***: **f** and **ph** are both used to denote a similar sound.
In "The Secret", the phrases "shining most stilly" and "singing most silently" are examples of alliteration.

1 How many examples of alliteration can you find in the poems? How do you think this enhances the poems?

I wander through each chartered street,
Near where the chartered Thames does flow,
And mark in every face I meet,
Marks of weakness, marks of woe.
In every cry of every man,
In every infant's cry of fear,
In every voice, in every ban,
The mind-forged manacles I hear:

How the chimney-sweeper's cry
Every blackening church appals,
And the hapless soldier's sigh
Runs in blood down palace-walls.

But most, through midnight streets I hear
How the youthful harlot's curse
Blasts the new-born infant's tear,
And blights with plagues the marriage-hearse.

—William Blake ("London")

Then, methought, the air grew denser, perfumed from an unseen censer
Swung by angels whose faint foot-falls tinkled on the tufted floor.
"Wretch," I cried, "thy God hath lent thee—by these angels he hath sent thee
Respite—respite and nepenthe from thy memories of Lenore!
Quaff, oh quaff this kind nepenthe and forget this lost Lenore!"
Quoth the raven, "Nevermore."

"Prophet!" said I, "thing of evil!—prophet still, if bird or devil!—
Whether Tempter sent, or whether tempest tossed thee here ashore,
Desolate yet all undaunted, on this desert land enchanted—
On this home by Horror haunted—tell me truly, I implore—
Is there—is there balm in Gilead?—tell me—tell me, I implore!"
Quoth the raven, "Nevermore."

"Prophet!" said I, "thing of evil—prophet still, if bird or devil!
By that Heaven that bends above us—by that God we both adore—
Tell this soul with sorrow laden if, within the distant Aidenn,

It shall clasp a sainted maiden whom the angels name Lenore—
Clasp a rare and radiant maiden whom the angels name Lenore."
Quoth the raven, "Nevermore."

—Edgar Allan Poe (from "The Raven")

2 In the poem "The Secret", certain phrases are used multiple times. Which phrases are these? Why do you think the poet uses them more than once?

Further Discussion

1 "The Purloined Letter" is one of the earliest detective stories. What do you think are the important elements of a detective story?

2 Read the story "The Blue Carbuncle" in the supplementary reader. Do you think the villains in either "The Blue Carbuncle" or "The Purloined Letter" are punished? Why or why not?

3 What does "The Purloined Letter" tell you about the character of Minister D? What do you think is Dupin's opinion of him?

Listening and Speaking

Do you think you could be a good detective? Play a game of "Twenty Questions" in class. One of your classmates will choose a subject (a person or thing) but will not reveal it to the others. The others must ask him or her up to twenty questions which can be answered with "yes" or "no" only. The first person to guess the answer becomes the person who chooses the secret subject for the next round.

Learn More

Find out which authors wrote the following famous mystery stories.

The Woman in White
Lady Audley's Secret
The Maltese Falcon
Gaudy Night
The Rilloby Fair Mystery
The Sign of Four
The Murder of Roger Ackroyd
Emil and the Detectives

The Future

"And in today already walks tomorrow."
—Samuel Taylor Coleridge

16 The World in Your Room

***Dr Mike Goldsmith** is a scientist and has written more than twenty non-fiction books for children. This chapter is adapted from his book* Fantastic Future.

If you're reading this in your bedroom, have a look round. If you're lucky, you'll see books and magazines, a mobile, a PC with email and internet access, a TV, radio, various remote controls, maybe a few postcards and photos—in other words, your room is stuffed to bursting with communication devices.

Over the last few centuries, a big chunk of the inventions people have come up with have been related in some ways to communication, from posting letters to sending texts. Communicating is something that people have always wanted to do. You were trying to do it as soon as you were born and well before you learned how (and very irritating for your parents it was too). You'll probably spend the rest of your life talking, phoning, writing, emailing and texting thousands of people.

Our keenness to communicate means that, in a few years, your bedroom might look something like this:

1. Super-mobile phones

Every so often in your future bedroom, your mobile will beep for attention and then tell you that your favorite band is about to start their **gig**. You'll send a quick text to those of your friends who like that band (your mobile will know which friends these are), and you'll be able to see and hear their performance—also on your mobile, which will record the best bits for later, too.

Today, almost everyone who can afford a mobile has got one, so, to go on selling them, the manufacturers have to keep coming up with new **gizmos**.

---

gig: a live performance by a musician or group playing popular or jazz music

gizmos: gadgets

A few decades further in the future, and you won't have to fish your mobile out from the back of the sofa—it'll be constantly at your side (or more likely on your shoulder or perched on—or even in—your ear). By then, computer memory will be so cheap your mobile will record everything that happens to you—everything you see and hear so you'll be able to look back over what happened during the last day, or decade: whenever you like. Clever software will be included, to gloss over the boring bits, not to mention those terribly embarrassing moments you'd rather draw a **discreet** veil over.

Mobiles like this will be very useful and not just for you. They'll download their information to the Internet, where all sorts of people will be able to access it—so tracking down criminals, finding missing persons, and getting instant ready made news bulletins will be easy. In fact, they'll be so useful that, chances are, mobiles will become compulsory one day.

2. Thought-controlled lights

These sound very science fictionish, but actually the way they'll work isn't all that complicated:

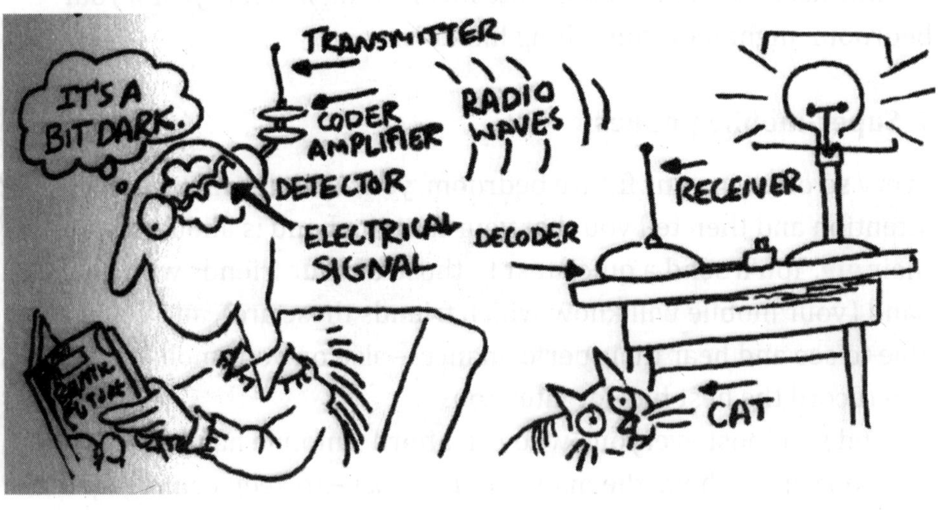

discreet: careful and prudent in one's speech or actions, especially in order to keep something confidential or to avoid embarrassment

Imagine a whole world of thought-controlled gadgets that will work just like this. As well as inventions that respond to instructions that we deliberately "think" at them there will be some that sense our mood. Some of your bedroom furniture will even think! Like...

3. Mind-reading bed/chair

Your future bedroom might be a bit smaller than today's, what with house prices rising and the population growing. So instead of a bed, easy chair and office-type chair, you may have just one thing—maybe it'll be called a Smart Chair, or perhaps a Ched or a Bair (actually, to be brutally honest, it might be called a Thunker for all I know—predicting what it's called is harder than predicting how it works). Anyway, imagine you've just finished your homework and it's time to listen to some music. Even as you think so, your "Ched" softens and reclines. Music comes out of it until you start to get sleepy, and the music softens and dies as the Ched gets wider and flatter and softer. It warms up a little, folds itself gently around and you fall peacefully sleep ...

How does it work? Well your brain produces regular patterns of electricity all the times, which depends on how you feel—these patterns change when you're alert, tired or asleep. Cheds will have built in detectors that will pick up and recognise these patterns. When your Ched notices that you're sleepy, it will turn into a bed, and when you're ready for homework, it will be too. When you're ready to get up, the Ched will be able to straighten gradually into a column—and then fold itself neatly away. Your Ched will have to "think"—to decide whether you really want to sleep, work, relax, or get up, based on the time, what you're doing, your usual pattern of behaviour and all sorts of things.

4. Carpet that cares

This is a bit like your Ched in that it will change to suit you, but it will react to physical signs rather than thoughts—it will be snuggly and warm on a cold winter's morning, smooth and cool on a June afternoon. It will also solve that awful problem: do you let your parents into your room to clean it, do it yourself, or let it get dirty? This carpet will keep itself clean—and the rest of the room too—by absorbing dust from the air. All this could be done by a network of narrow tubes down which cool or warm air is blown, or dust is sucked. The carpet will also act as a burglar alarm if someone steps on it when you've told it you're out. Perhaps carpets like this could even trap burglars like flies in a web, by squirting a network of sticky threads over them that harden in the air.

5. Virtual Reality system

Virtual Reality (VR) involves a computer producing sounds, images and physical sensations so realistic that they can convince us that they're real. It's not as easy as it seems, because what we sense depends on how we move. Also, even the best VR systems around today don't generate smell or tastes and physical sensations are limited to a few **prods** and presses on the inside surface of a glove you wear, or some jerks and wobbles of your chair. The easiest bit of a VR system to get to work is the audio system—stereo headphones are all you need, and they were around even before your parents were your age, practically for ever, in other words. Getting a realistic picture isn't too difficult either—for a three-dimensional effect, all you need is two tiny screens that show slightly different views, one for each eye.

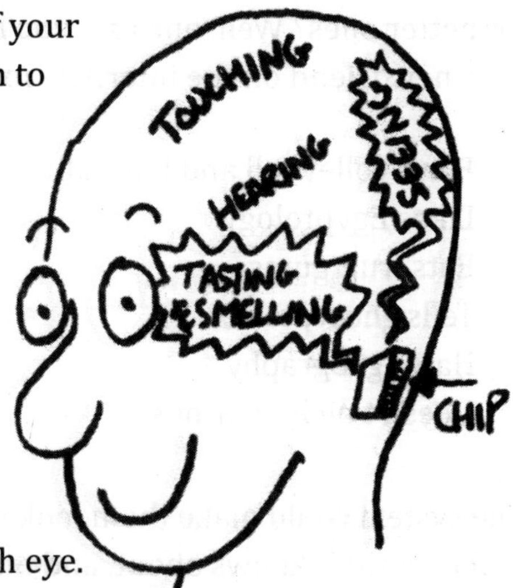

Of course, when thought technology takes off, all this equipment will seem as outdated as a suit of armour. Just a little chip attached to your head—or surgically implanted into it—might do it all feeding signals directly to the parts of your brain you use for seeing, hearing, touching, tasting and smelling.

6. Rewritable books

In your futuristic bedroom, you might have only one book. At the press of a button—or a spoken word from you—its pages will change from a comic to a history book (when it's time to do your homework), and then maybe to a TV guide, A to Z, or the latest title, depending on what sort of evening you have in mind. Rewritable books like this will look like ordinary books, but with thicker, glossier pages. Each

---

prods: pokes with a finger, foot or pointed object

page will have thousands of tiny spheres embedded in it. The spheres will be white on top and black underneath. When the book receives a computer file of data, some spheres will turn over, making black dots appear in groups, forming letters and pictures.

7. Your virtual friend

Have you ever tired of your friends and wished you could swap them for better ones? Well, one day, you'll be able to. Imagine you're looking for a new friend on the internet. You might want someone who:

Plays volleyball and football
Likes Egyptology
Eats fruit gums
Tells ghost stories
Hates geography
Doesn't pick their nose

The system could make them look through its register of all the people in the world it knows about, and offer you a likely new friend. Or, if there's no one suitable, it makes one for you! There are plenty of primitive versions of such friends—called Chatbots—on the internet already. At the moment all they can do is respond to what you type in a way that, for a short time, might convince you that they are a real person. It's likely that, in a decade or less, they will be very much more realistic—perhaps with real-looking faces, voices you can hear and intelligence and emotions, too. And you'll be able to speak to them rather than typing messages.

Reading Comprehension

1 Answer the following questions.
   i What are some of the communication devices that may be found in an ordinary home?
   ii Why must manufacturers of mobile phones keep coming up with new devices?
   iii Why might bedrooms in the future be smaller?
   iv What is a "Ched"? Why will it have to think?
   v What does VR stand for? What does it mean?
   vi What are "Chatbots"?

Vocabulary

1 Match the following authors with the names of the books about the future that they wrote.

George Orwell	Foundation
Ray Bradbury	Brave New World
Aldous Huxley	Farenheit 451
H.G. Wells	1984
Isaac Asimov	When the Sleeper Wakes

Grammar

Split Infinitives

Where infinitives are used, ideally there should not be any words between the "to" and the simple form of the verb. Such a situation (where one or more words divide the infinitive) is known as a **split infinitive**. ***For example***: the tagline of the TV series Star Trek, "to boldly go where no man has gone before" is a split infinitive (it could be rewritten as "to go boldly..."). Split infinitives are not really bad grammar but they are usually best avoided.

1 Rewrite the following sentences removing the split infinitive.

i Kanika was able to easily pass the maths exam, though she had trouble with geography and Sanskrit.

ii The best thing about weekends is that you're able to not wake up early.

iii My brother always manages to cleverly forget that it's his turn to make the breakfast.

iv His neighbour has a tendency to loudly play music in the middle of the night.

v It's natural to sometimes forget important dates but you really should apologise to your sister for forgetting her birthday.

vi Siddharth's look of boredom made it clear that he wanted to immediately leave.

Writing

This chapter suggests a number of gadgets that it might be possible to have in the future. What invention or gadget would you like to see in the near future? Write a paragraph describing it and the ways in which it might be useful to you.

17 There Will Come Soft Rains

***Sara Teasdale** (1884–1933) was an American poet.*

There will come soft rains and the smell of the ground,
And swallows circling with their
shimmering sound;

And frogs in the pool singing at night,
And wild plum trees in **tremulous**
white;

Robins will wear their feathery
fire,
Whistling their **whims** on a low
fence-wire;

And not one will know of the war,
not one
Will care at last when it is done.

Not one would mind, neither bird nor tree,
If mankind perished utterly;

And Spring herself when she woke at dawn
Would scarcely know that we were gone.

---

tremulous: shaking or quivering slightly
whims: sudden desires or change of mind, especially one that is unusual or unexplained

Reading Comprehension

1 Answer the following questions.

i What has happened to mankind in this poem?

ii How do you think this has happened?

iii Do the animals and birds care that men no longer exist? Why do you think this is?

iv What do the last two lines tell us about our place in the world?

Vocabulary

Pathetic Fallacy

Pathetic fallacy means depicting non-living objects or concepts as if they had human emotions and thoughts. In the poem "There Will Come Soft Rains", the following lines are an example of pathetic fallacy:

"And Spring herself when she woke at dawn
Would scarcely know that we were gone."

Here Spring is depicted as a living being that wakes and sleeps like humans and is capable of knowing things.

1 Read these extracts from poems and identify the instances of pathetic fallacy in them.

i And they tell me you are brutal and my reply is: On the faces of women and children I have seen the marks of wanton hunger.
And having answered so I turn once more to those who sneer at this my city, and I give them back the sneer and say to them:

Come and show me another city with lifted head singing
so proud to be alive and coarse and strong and cunning.
Flinging magnetic curses amid the toil of piling job on
job, here is a tall bold slugger set vivid against the
little soft cities;

—Carl Sandburg ("Chicago")

ii Earth hath not anything to show more fair:
Dull would he be of soul who could pass by
A sight so touching in its majesty:
This City now doth, like a garment, wear
The beauty of the morning; silent, bare,
Ships, towers, domes, theatres and temples lie
Open unto the fields, and to the sky;
All bright and glittering in the smokeless air.

—William Wordsworth
("Composed Upon Westminster Bridge...")

iii In the stormy east-wind straining,
The pale yellow woods were waning,
The broad stream in his banks complaining,
Heavily the low sky raining
Over tower'd Camelot;
Down she came and found a boat
Beneath a willow left afloat,
And round about the prow she wrote
'The Lady of Shalott.'

—Alfred, Lord Tennyson ("The Lady of Shalott")

18 The Story Collector

Kuzhali Manickavel *is an Indian writer of short stories. She has lived in India and Canada. She is best known for her collection of short stories,* Insects Are Just like You and Me except Some of Them Have Wings.

Skanda watched the first Sulphur fumes rise into the sky like thin, yellow fingers. The day was about to end.

Warning sirens began blaring overhead, which meant that the gates to the underground Tunnels that ran in and out of each other and to the cities, were closing. He would have to find another way back to MetroDome.

It had been many centuries since anything had been able to survive on the Surface of the Earth. Even in the daytime the Surface was covered with hot, bitter clouds of smoke that rose from the Sulphur pits. Urchins like Skanda braved the heat and noxious fumes to scavenge the scrap heaps. But at night the Sulphur coated the Surface in thick, yellow billows that made it impossible for anything to survive.

Skanda ran into the nearest ruined building. His lungs were burning from the Sulphur. He felt his eyes water and his nostrils burn with each breath he took.

As he sprinted along the crumbling hallway, Skanda spotted a gaping hole under a flight of broken stairs. He dived in. He felt himself falling, bouncing off rough, earthy walls until he landed with a thud on a warm dirt floor. Something was poking into his back, a thin, rectangular piece of ... rock? No, it was softer than a rock.

Skanda fished into his pocket for his Glostick. Perhaps he had landed on an abandoned Platinum Kit or an old MicaPad. He turned and held his Glostick up.

Skanda pinched himself. He *had* to be dreaming.

He had landed on a book.

Books did not exist in Skanda's world. Long ago, the Grand Ministry of MetroDome had filed them under the NotNeeded Department, the department for things that were not useful to the growth and prosperity of the city. Books were considered extremely NotNeeded because they stopped people from hammering nails or driving buses or adding numbers. The only words that people read in MetroDome, apart from official ones, were AdWords and NewsWords, which continually streamed past as they boarded their trains, drank their coffee or went shopping. As for writing—nobody had held a pen in centuries. People keyed words in with zero-error KeyPads that used a standardised list of government-approved WordsandPhrases.

The only person who had ever actually seen a book was an old, old woman Skanda had gone **scavenging** with a long time ago. Books, she had told him, were the most wonderful things; they had leaves of paper filled with hundreds and hundreds of words that stood perfectly still. They were a magic way to escape; if you had a book, you could go anywhere at all.

Reading the book was a bit hard at first. Skanda spent some time looking for the power switch until he remembered that the words would not move. Following the words was a bit tricky too, since he kept expecting them to **stream** across the page. But in the end he got the hang of it and managed to read the whole book.

It was a collection of stories from the time when people were scattered all over the surface of the planet. The writer had travelled far and wide, collecting stories as he went. I wish I could do that, Skanda thought. What could be better than travelling and collecting stories? But Skanda had never been anywhere except MetroDome and the dumping grounds. More importantly, he didn't know the first thing about stories.

One afternoon, after a fruitless day of scavenging in a scrap iron heap, Skanda came across a pile of soft lead pieces. One merchant in MetroDome gave a stale bun in exchange for two handfuls of soft lead pieces. Skanda began breaking the lead pieces against the nearest wall.

---

scavenging: searching for and collecting (anything usable) from discarded waste

stream: a continuous flow of something

The lead left dark markings on the greyish surface; some looked like full-stops while others looked like dashes.

Skanda picked up a sharp piece of lead and drew a line on the wall. Then he drew another line, and, with great concentration, a funny face. Then he had an idea.

Skanda began to practice writing letters on the walls of the ruined buildings. He kept getting the small "d" and "b" mixed up, and his "s"s kept squiggling in the wrong direction, but soon he was able to write words that actually looked like words. He began to cover the walls of the ruined buildings with any word that caught his fancy—"fish", "**grandeur**", "adhesive", "**orthodontist**".

Skanda still wished he had a story that would put his words to use.

One late afternoon, he was so preoccupied with the story he didn't have that he didn't feel his hand slip into his pocket and fish out a lump of lead. He barely noticed when his hands began to move, forming a string of words on the wall of an underground Tunnel ...

Mole, a Regulation Grade Q Painter of Crossings (White Enamel Paint), was going home after another day of work. He always walked through the Tunnels thinking of his job or his lunch or his shoes. He barely noticed the AdWords or NewsWords that flashed by him every day, and he hardly ever read them. But that evening, he noticed that a certain set of words *weren't* **skimming** past him. They certainly weren't **regulation** WordsandPhrases from the KeyPads; how had they leaked onto the walls? For the very first time in his life, Mole slowed down and paused to read.

Once there lived a boy who could make words come out of his hand. He could write words all day, covering the walls and floors with anything that came to his head. One day, the boy decided that he wanted to write stories.

And so he set out to find one.

grandeur: splendour and impressiveness, especially of appearance or style
orthodontist: doctor who specialises in the treatment of irregularities in the teeth and jaws

skimming: move quickly and lightly over or on a surface or through the air
regulation: of the correct type

Every day, the string of words kept growing. Mole found himself looking forward to his walks home so he could read what had been added.

"It's the most extraordinary thing," he said to his wife. "It's about a boy who makes words with his hands and goes out into the world to find a story."

Mole's wife stared. "Why does he want to find a story? Where is he going to find one?"

Mole shrugged. "We'll have to keep reading to find out."

Mole began to copy the words down to show his wife how the story had grown. At first, he tried using his KeyPad but it kept rejecting the non-standardised sets of words. In the end, he used some of his paint and the thinnest brush he could find, on sheets from a stack of brown wrapping paper, and began to copy the markings by hand. It wasn't as easy as it looked but after a few days, Mole finally got the hang of it. At home, Mole's wife read the growing story and showed it to her friends in the neighborhood.

Once Skanda began to write about his hunt for stories, he found he could not stop. And he found that the words just came to him once he had the lead in his hand. At first, they came slowly, but then they came so fast that his hands could barely keep up.

He wrote about the old woman who had told him about books and the noises that the Sulphur pits made if you threw lead pieces into them. He wrote about the time he had found two lumps of Aluminium in one day and about the boy who said he felt drops of water fall from the sky once when he was wandering on the Surface.

Skanda didn't think of them as stories—they were just thoughts, ideas, feelings and words that ran through his head and on to the walls. He would scavenge all afternoon, and once people had gone home after work, he would creep into the Tunnels and wait for them to shut. After that, it was quiet and he could work by the light of his Glostick. When the blaring of sirens signalled the opening of the Tunnels in the morning, Skanda would slip out quietly and find a place to sleep.

One day the
king set out
see his

Mole and his wife weren't the only ones following the story. The **novelty** of the words that didn't move and the boy who collected stories attracted tens, and then hundreds of people to the Tunnel. Some came to read the story from the very beginning while others came to catch up on what had been added. Just like Mole, there were other people who copied the story down to show their family and friends.

By the time Skanda's story had extended into its fifth Tunnel, seven written volumes of his story were circulating about the city and being updated every day. As no one knew who the creator of these words was, he came to be known as the Story Collector.

It wasn't long before news of the Story Collector reached MetroHall, the political centre of MetroDome. After much tossing back and forth, the matter finally landed in the WorkPod of the City Commissioner. He TeleConned the head of Tunnel Security for an assessment.

"It's by the Story Collector, Mr Commissioner. It's all stationary, sir, doesn't move or anything. It's about this boy who can make words, and he goes looking for a story and ..."

"Yes, but what exactly is the problem?" snapped the Commissioner.

"Problem? Why, there's no problem, just a lot of people coming in and reading the story and enjoying ..."

"Arrest anyone caught making words in the Tunnels. Shut them up for life. And repaint the Tunnels."

"But sir ..."

"The Commissioner has spoken!" And he banged the TeleCon down, feeling very proud of himself.

Skanda was arrested the following morning as he left the Tunnel, though it was the oddest arrest you ever saw. All the men of Tunnel Security were very keen followers of the story and were thrilled to finally meet the real Story Collector face to face. Skanda was given the best cell in the block, complete with a supply of lead so that he could write on the walls whenever he felt like it. He was a bit

---

novelty: the quality of being new, original or unusual

confused about what was happening, and it was difficult to stay awake during the day.

Meanwhile, news that the Story Collector had been arrested swept through the city like fire. Why would anyone want to arrest the Story Collector? There was no crime in writing stories that everyone enjoyed! There was a lot of grumbling and muttering that spread through MetroDome.

The next day, the Commissioner was about to settle into his first nap of the morning when the door of his office suddenly flew open. Staring down at him was the Supreme Head of the Grand Ministry and he was looking particularly sour.

"I suppose you've been too busy to have a look outside your window," he hissed.

The Commissioner peered outside from the fortieth floor of the towering MetroHall and nearly swallowed his tongue. MetroDome looked empty. There was almost no one in the streets, at the bus stops, in any of the shops or in any of the offices. Even the houses wore a **deserted** look.

"Is it plague? Are they all dead?" asked the Commissioner.

"Oh no, they're fine. In fact, they're striking in front of the Tunnels."

"Why? What for?"

"BECAUSE YOU ARRESTED THE STORY COLLECTOR, YOU IDIOT!"

"But..."

"SHUT UP!" roared the Supreme Head. "Do you have any idea how much this strike is costing the city?"

"Yes, sir. I mean ..."

"So what are you going to do about it, Mr Commissioner?"

He swallowed hard. "I'm ... going to release the Story Collector?"

"And?"

"I ... will cancel the order to repaint the Tunnels?"

"And?"

"I ... will submit my resignation?"

"Now that's the best idea you've had your entire career! I shall

---

deserted: empty of people

mention it at your farewell party."

The Supreme Head disappeared.

Skanda was sitting in his private cell, staring blankly at his lead supply. There were a million different thoughts and feelings seesawing within him. On the one hand, he had been arrested for no reason. On the other, he was sitting on the nicest bed he had ever been on in his entire life, and getting three free meals a day. They had even served ice cream after dinner! There was a feeling of **exultation** that so many people had read and enjoyed his stories, but he hadn't realised that the story would cause him problems. What if they sent him to the mines? What if he was jailed for life?

"Psst!"

Skanda looked up and saw a pale-faced young man signalling to him from the next cell.

"Thinking of your next story?" asked the man.

Skanda shook his head and sighed. "Wish I'd never started writing. It got me arrested and they might keep me here forever. And I heard that there's all sorts of trouble happening outside because of me."

The man laughed. "You know what I'm in here for, Story Collector? I've been arrested for the unlawful manufacture of flutes. Bet you don't even know what that is."

Skanda shook his head again.

"It's something you make music with. There isn't a sweeter sound in the whole world."

"But why would they arrest you for that?"

The man shrugged. "Because it makes people stop and listen. And you know what? As soon as they let me out, I'm going to make another one and I'm going to play it until they arrest me again. I've been in here two hundred and seventy-eight times already."

"Wow," said Skanda. It seemed like a very noble reason to keep going to jail.

"And as for you, Story Collector, I'm afraid that even if they do let you out you'll just keep on writing and keep coming back here, like

---

exultation: a feeling of triumphant elation or jubilation; rejoicing me. That's just how we are. So, like I said, are you thinking of your next story?"

Skanda felt a great lump of sadness rise to his throat. "I haven't got any more stories. And now they've locked me up and I'll never be able to find another one," he said mournfully.

The man snapped his fingers. "Good God, here you are, sitting with the only flute-maker in all of MetroDome, who just told you all about his two-hundred-and-seventy-ninth trip to jail and you say you have nothing to write about?"

And Skanda realised that he had just collected his next story.

After lunch, Skanda was released and driven under police escort to the Tunnels where he was asked to continue writing. Everyone went back to work, after being assured that the next installment of the story would be ready and waiting on the walls when the day was over.

Skanda's story was declared an official MetroDome Monument with reading tours conducted twice a day. It would take five years, but eventually, the NotNeeded Department was declared null and void, and flutes, books, paintings and bubblegum, among many other things, were made legal.

As it turned out, Skanda had many more stories to tell. Some were whispered to him by the echoes in the Tunnels. Others were ones he heard from people chatting on the bus or arguing in restaurants. Still others were found hidden in the most unlikely places: on a street corner, in the neighbourhood grocery store or in the sound of the pale young man playing his flute. Each story seemed to be waiting for Skanda like a fistful of sparkling gems hidden in a lump of ordinary coal.

And Skanda always found them. After all, he was the Story Collector.

Reading Comprehension

1 Answer the following questions.

i What did Skanda do for a living?

ii Why didn't anyone live on the surface of the earth?

iii Why were books considered NotNeeded?

iv What drew Mole's attention to the story?

v Who gave Skanda the title of The Story Collector? Why?

vi Who was the pale-faced young man? What realisation did Skanda come to after speaking to him?

vii Why was Skanda released from prison?

Vocabulary

Neologism

Science fiction stories like "The Story Collector" often use newly coined words or **neologisms**, to express ideas. Neologisms are frequently made by combining two or more already-existing words.
For example: the word "cyberspace" is a combination of existing words "cybernetics" and "space". It was coined by the author William Gibson in his book *Neuromancer*.

1 Read the chapter and make a complete list of the neologisms used. Why do you think the author does this?

Writing

In the chapter "What is My Single Life Worth" you read about the practice of banning books. In "The Story Collector" a boy is arrested for collecting and writing stories. What about stories and books do you think is so important? Why do you think that writers of books are so often challenged or silenced? Write a short essay detailing your thoughts.

Further Discussion

1 In the chapters in this section, do you think the vision of the future is a positive or negative one?

2 Why do you think the author of "The Story Collector" focuses on the power of books and music?

3 Compare the poem "There Will Come Soft Rains" to the short story of the same name in the Literature Reader.

4 Do you think that the poem "There Will Come Soft Rains" says anything about humans' effects upon the environment?

5 Both "The World in Your Room" and "The Story Collector" describe the possibility of reading books on electronic devices. Do you think that e-books are a positive development? Why or why not?

Listening and Speaking

Find out more about any issue that you think will have a big impact on the future of our world. Give a short report about it in class. Some of the topics you could choose are:

i Global warming
ii Advances in technology
iii E-books
iv Pollution
v Population

Learn More

1 Doomsday Theories

"Eschatology" comes from the Greek word eschatos, meaning "last". It means the study of the end of the world. Many cultures or religions have stories about how the world will end. Find out more about the following theories about the end of the world.

Ragnarok
Frashnokereti
The 2012 Phenomenon
Yawm al-Qiyāmah
The Planet X or Nibiru Collision
Kali Yuga
Armageddon
The Big Crunch

2 Find out the meanings of the following words:
Utopia
Dystopia

Which of the two words do you think more accurately describes our future? Why?

Acknowledgements

The publishers would like to thank the following authors, illustrators and publishers for permission to use their materials:
Subrata Guha for permission to use an extract from *Mahabharata: The War* by Soma Guha (Scholastic India: 2007); Anjali Nayar for the illustration for "Music"; Baaraan Ijlal for the illustration for "There Will Come Soft Rains"; Kunal Kundu for the illustrations for "Friendship Sonnet", "The Purloined Letter", "My Last Duchess" and "The Story Collector"; Kuzhali Manickavel for "The Story Collector" from *Seven Science Fiction Stories* (Scholastic India: 2006); Leslee Lazar for "The Power of Hearing" from *The Five Senses* (Scholastic India: 2008); Nilima Eriyat for the illustrations for "Under a Telephone Pole" and "The Battle of Blenheim"; Partha Sengupta for the illustrations for "The Power of Hearing"; Priya Kuriyan for the illustrations for "Yogurt and Cinnamon Dessert with Rose Geraniums and Peach"; Priyankar Gupta for the illustrations for "The Happy Prince", "Talking to Jason"; Rehan Ansari for "27 Nisbat Road" from *City Stories* (Scholastic India: 2007); Salman Rushdie for "What is My Single Life Worth?" from *The Rushdie Letters: Freedom to Speak, Freedom to Write* edited by Steve MacDonogh (Brandon Book Publishers: 1993); Sampurna Chattarji for "Yogurt and Cinnamon Dessert with Rose Geraniums and Peach" from *The Fried Frog and Other Funny Freaky Foodie Feisty Poems* (Scholastic India: 2009); Sharada Bhanu, Padma Malini Raghavan and Padma Seshadri for "Two Myths About Fire" from *103 Myths, Legends, Fables and Stuff* (Scholastic India: 2008); Scholastic UK for "The World in

Your Room" from *Fantastic Future* (Scholastic UK: 2004); Scholastic US for "Talking to Jason" from *Rules* by Cynthia Lord (Scholastic US: 2006) and "The Purloined Letter" from *Mystery Plays* by Tom Conklin (Scholastic US: 2007); Taposhi Ghoshal for the illustration for "Two Myths About Fire"; Zainab Tambawalla for the illustration for "What is My Single Life Worth?".

While every attempt has been made to trace copyright holders for the text and illustrations, this has not been possible in all cases. Any omissions brought to our attention will be rectified in future editions.

Evaluation Table

Name: ____________________

Date: ____________________

THEME	Comprehension	Grammar, Spelling and Punctuation	Vocabulary	Organisation of Ideas	Making Connections	Expression
Friendship						
Communication						
The World						
Art and Culture						
War and Peace						
Mysteries						
The Future						